D1637507

A guide to the West Highland Way

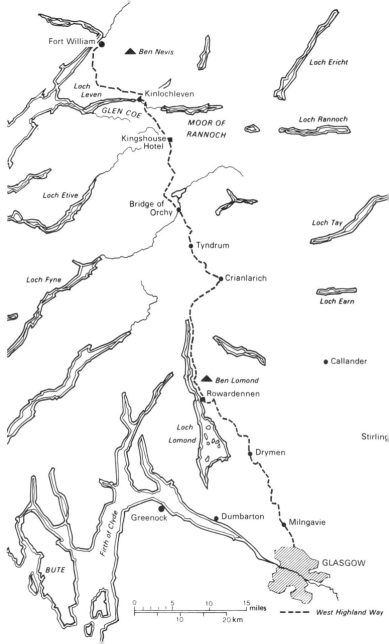

Fort William
Ben Nevis
Loch Ericht
Loch Leven
Kinlochleven
GLEN COE
MOOR OF RANNOCH
Loch Rannoch
Kingshouse Hotel
Loch Etive
Bridge of Orchy
Loch Tay
Tyndrum
Loch Fyne
Crianlarich
Loch Earn
Callander
Ben Lomond
Rowardennen
Loch Lomond
Stirling
Drymen
Firth of Clyde
Greenock
Dumbarton
Milngavie
GLASGOW
BUTE

0   5   10   15 miles
0   10   20 km
- - - West Highland Way

A guide to

The West Highland Way

Tom Hunter

Photographs by
W.A. Poucher, Hon F.R.P.S.

Foreword by
John Hillaby

Constable London

First published in Great Britain 1979
by Constable and Company Limited
3 The Lanchesters, 162 Fulham Palace Road,
London W6 9ER
Copyright © 1979 by Tom Hunter
Reprinted 1980
Second edition 1984
Reprinted 1988
Reprinted 1992
Reprinted 1995
ISBN 0 09 469090 1
Printed in Great Britain by
BAS Printers Ltd,
Over Wallop, Hampshire

To Diana
'The mistress of mountains and forests green, lonely glades
and sounding rivers'

Contents

Sron na Creise with Kingshouse Hotel in foreground

Illustrations

Maps

Foreword
by John Hillaby
(President of the Backpackers Club)

Years and years ago I was driven down the length of the Great Glen by a bustling scout-master who, for quite the wrong sort of reasons, said that I would never forget the experience. Nowadays I wonder, sometimes, whether my youthful companions still recall the downpours called mist and the seemingly endless corduroy of conifers that clothe the lower end of that famous geological fault. Loch Ness and Loch Lochy have plenty to offer on a fine day. But they are much of a muchness, and it was not until we neared Fort William that I sensed something of the grandeur of the west. All that took place close on half a century ago. No guide books were easily available in those days. But here, with abundant information about how to use it, is the key to that great door to adventure. I consider this to be a most important book.

At the risk of rough reprisals from clansmen around the Cairngorms, I claim that no landscapes throughout the whole of Britain have more to offer the walker in the way of spectacular variety than the Western Highlands. The scenery has been sculptured out of solid rock. In places the great ridge of Drum Albyn, the jagged spine of the west, rises almost sheer from the sea, Variety comes from the fact that the ridge has been slashed by the rivers and glaciers of long ago. The glens and sea lochs are the outcome of ice and water and, earlier still, of volcanic fires that smouldered deep beneath the thin, senile soil. The glens are wild. They have given the country character. They are a little awesome if you don't know what you are about. Who, then, can act as a reliable guide?

We are particularly fortunate to have obtained the services of Tom Hunter, a dedicated walker and a pioneer of the West Highland Way, a man whose professional business is with organisation and method. Before you set off with this guide readily available in the side pocket of your rucksack, I hope you will devote more than a little time of what he has to say about rights of way, safety precautions, mountain rescue, and books that will give you much to think about along the route he recommends.

I have for long contended that when you are out and about in the open air, if you don't know something about what you are looking for, you can't be expected to look at it for very long. The Highlands are by far the wildest part of the British Isles. The last wolf was said to have been killed in Invernessshire in 1743. The actual date is unimportant: what matters is that the great pine forests of Caledon were burned to the ground to restrict its range. And to smoke out banditry and lay the way open for the coming of the sheep, one of the most important and tragic factors in the history of the spoliation of Scotland, a process largely brought about by the stark cupidity of Southerners. Before that fateful period, the soft pastures of the glens were selectively grazed and fertilised by superbly adapted cattle. In countless thousands they were driven south into the stomachs of the English along the drove roads, examples of which may be plainly seen on Rannoch Moor and elsewhere. On the high tops were flocks of ptarmigan and eagles watching from their eyries. In the forest below roamed red deer, now forced to migrate out in the open. All this and much more you may read in *The Highlands and Islands* by Frank Fraser Darling and John Morton Boyd (see the Bibliography).

If you are not a Scot you would be wise to look out for important Gaelic words on your maps, words such as *creag* meaning crag or cliff, and *coire*, a blind valley or corrie that almost always leads you nowhere except, often, to a *creag* on the other side. 'Ben' or its Gaelic equivalent *beinn* is, of course, a hill which may be *mor* (big), *beg* (small), *dubh* (black), *rhuadh* (red) and very often glas (grey). Mr Hunter has provided us with a glossary. Safety and comfort are matters of uncommon sense. Remember always that it's almost as important to keep cool as it is to keep warm. Hyperthermia is nearly as dangerous as hypothermia. Wear clothes that can be zipped up or zipped down.

The Pennine Way, the path that runs across ten sheets of the Ordnance Survey, is probably the best-known track in Britain. We hope it will soon be linked up to the West Highland Way by an approved and satisfying route across the burghs of the Border; and then, with a northern extension to this trail, it will be possible to walk from Edale in Derbyshire to Cape Wrath in Sutherland.

Meanwhile, with this guide to hand, you may safely venture into a realm of almost inexpressible beauty.

In 1968 the Countryside Commission for Scotland set up sub-committees to examine and report on two aspects of the countryside: 1) Footpaths and Long Distance Routes and 2) Wilderness Areas in Scotland. The bulk of this research dealt with the Highland areas, and it was the late Alex Gray – an Honorary President of the Glasgow Group of the Holiday Fellowship – who suggested that similar work should be undertaken round Glasgow and the bordering counties.

On 10 March 1969, Alex Gray convened a meeting of his club at Strathclyde University and two sub-committees were elected – one to consider Open Space Conservation around Glasgow and the other to study the creation of public paths and long-distance walking routes linking the towns and villages in Dunbartonshire, Lanarkshire, Renfrewshire and Stirlingshire with the countryside within and outside these counties.

Since I have always been interested in long-distance walking I volunteered to serve on the sub-committee dealing with this aspect, and although the terms of the remit were enormous, I reluctantly accepted the convenorship of this sub-committee. At a later date and at my suggestion, the sub-committee decided to concentrate on the idea of one long-distance walking route from Glasgow to the north. The final terminal was undecided at that time.

The task of surveying the best route seemed formidable and it was agreed to invite other walking organisations to join us. Invitations were sent to all the principal walking clubs of Glasgow – Countrywide Holidays Association, Glenmore Club, Health Culture and Ramblers' Association. It was very pleasing to find that those organisations were interested and sent representatives to the later meetings; they also agreed it was best to concentrate all our efforts in pioneering a long-distance route north from Glasgow. The inspiration was the success of the Pennine Way – Tom Stephenson had established the first long route in England; why, we then thought, could we not have the second in Scotland?

While all this preliminary work was proceeding, other interested parties were taking a hand in shaping the future of the route. The city of Glasgow was being re-developed and during that time the policy of the Parks Department was being changed under the dynamic leadership of the then Parks Director, Mr Arthur Oldham. With the Glasgow Parks Convenor, Councillor Hutcheson, he was thinking of linking the city with the countryside by means of walkways through the public parks.

After a series of articles had appeared in the press, members of our committee suggested this was perhaps a good time to contact Mr Oldham and inform him of our own ideas. He was extremely interested and from then on I received tremendous encouragement and help from him. By now our surveys were actively under way and Fort William had been chosen as the northern terminal, with the hope that the sub-committee from the Countryside Commission would in future link the route with other Highland route-ways.

Each club representative was given a territorial division of the area to be surveyed. Separate survey parties from his organisation reported their findings to him. From their advice concerning the best routing of a section, he was able to report to the sub-committee on the territory allotted to his organisation.

The entire summer of 1969 was devoted to this task of surveying, and we plotted the best route – in our opinion – north from Glasgow to Fort William. In January 1970, I presented a draft report to the Glasgow Group of Holiday Fellowship, and in February 1970 Alex Gray further submitted the report to the Scottish Countryside Activities Council and the Countryside Commission for Scotland.

Also about this time the Scottish Development Department had appointed an outside consultant, Mr F.J. Evans, to undertake a Pilot Footways Study in the Glasgow area and its environs, and his report was published in May 1970. We had submitted our survey maps to Mr Evans in order that he could incorporate the entire route from the Kelvin Way to Glen Falloch. It was he who named the route 'The Highland Way', later to be changed by the Countryside Commission to 'The West Highland Way' to ensure the title did not prejudice the names of further long-distance routes in the Highlands.

The Countryside Commission's comprehensive report on the West Highland Way was issued in December 1973, and presented to the Secretary of State for Scotland who approved the scheme in September 1974. It now rests with the local authorities to implement the proposals fully, but I understand the route may not be opened officially until 1980. However sections of the route can be walked now and I hope this guidebook will be useful until Scotland's first long-distance walking route is officially opened.

At present there are twelve approved long-distance routes in England and Wales, and many western European countries also have such routes. I agree with the Countryside Commission in their report when they say that increasing numbers of people are learning to appreciate this form of access, and this lends urgency to the need for the official creation of the West Highland Way.

I am indebted to Mr W.A. Poucher for his fine selection of photographs, and to Mr D.H. McPherson for his invaluable advice on Rights of Way in Scotland.

I wish to thank my wife for assistance in the field, for checking the manuscript, and for her constant criticism which although annoying was very necessary.

Tom Hunter
1978

Since first publication, new wooden markers with Thistle Motif have been introduced on the route.

February 1980

From 1978 to 1980 the Countryside Commission for Scotland and the Local Authorities were determined to make the route a reality. Considerable assistance was given by units of the Regular and Territorial Army, by Forestry Commission staff and the British Trust for Conservation Volunteers in the construction of bridges, in drainage, path clearing, and way-marking.

The West Highland Way was officially opened to walkers by the Earl of Mansfield, Minister of State at the Scottish Office, on Monday 6 October 1980.

March 1984

It is well to be properly equipped and prepared for any type of weather. Experienced hill-walkers always take the Scottish hills seriously. In winter especially, the conditions can be Arctic and great care is required.

Most important, know how to use a map and compass. Carry a map of the area – the recommended Ordnance Survey maps 1 inch: 1 mile scale or the new metric 1:50,000 are listed below in respect of the West Highland Way. The most practical compass for mountain navigation is the Silva type. It is a good idea to be able to measure distances on the map and estimate the time any route will take. Naismith's Rule is a good rough guide – speed of walking is three miles an hour and an additional half-hour for each 1,000 feet of ascent. This speed is reduced when carrying a heavy load, and an estimate could be two and a half miles an hour plus one hour for every 1,500 feet of ascent. Additional allowances must be made for halts or bad weather.

A subject closely allied to safety is load-carrying. Keep the load as light as possible while still observing the other rules of mountain safety. Keep the weight of the load high and as directly above the spine as possible; this is much less tiring than having the weight hanging back from the shoulders. The modern 'high packs' keep this principle in mind. When packing, it is advisable to place lighter articles at the bottom and heavier articles at the top, but make sure that the load is well balanced because a badly packed rucksack can throw one off balance when crossing streams and in other awkward places.

The purchase of a large, thick polythene bag is a useful addition, as all articles of clothing and equipment can be packed in it and kept dry inside the rucksack. If you are stranded, the polythene bag can be used as an extra cover for warmth and protection from rain.

A useful little booklet called *Safety on Mountains*, published by the Central Council of Physical Recreation, 26 Park Crescent, London, W1, is well worth purchasing for its essential advice to hill-walkers and climbers.

Maps

Throughout this book, copies of Bartholomew maps scale 1:100,000 are reproduced but they should only be used as a general guide to sections of the route. In order to make a more detailed study and for actual way-finding, the walker on the West Highland Way is recommended to use the following sheets of the Ordnance Survey:

> The one-inch Tourist Maps 'Loch Lomond and the Trossachs' and 'Ben Nevis and Glencoe' cover the route from Milngavie to Fort William.

> For the entire route from Glasgow to Fort William: Seventh Series – 1 inch: 1 mile Nos 46, 47, 53, 54 and 60 or New Metric 1:50,000 Nos 41, 50, 56, 57 and 64

Advice for climbers

Although this book is primarily a guide to the West Highland Way, there are suggestions for climbs as diversions in some of the chapters. I would recommend the potential climber to read the excellent guide-books issued by the Scottish Mountaineering Club and W.A. Poucher's *The Scottish Peaks*, to acquaint himself with detailed routes and with other information about the particular hills which he wishes to climb.

Any climb which is perfectly safe and simple in good weather can be entirely different if the weather worsens, and such weather changes can occur very quickly on the Scottish hills. Enough time must be allowed for a hill-climbing expedition, especially when the route is new to the climber. A party should always leave information at its base (hotel, hostel or tent) about the party's intentions as to route and estimated time of return. This can save valuable hours of searching in the event of an accident.

Three is the minimum number to ensure safety should an accident occur. One member can remain with the injured person while the third member seeks assistance. The pace of climbing is dictated by the slowest member of the party and the party should always remain together.

All parties should carry simple first-aid equipment, torch, whistle, relevant Ordnance Survey Maps of the area (scale 1 inch: 1 mile or 1:50,000) and compass. Ice-axes should be carried if there is a chance of snow or ice, and you should be able to use the ice-axe properly.

Extra warm clothing should be carried at all times and also protective clothing for wet weather. Food to be carried varies according to taste but it is advisable to include food which can be quickly converted into energy – jams, sugar, chocolate, nuts and raisins. Alcohol is best avoided when out on the hills.

Mountain rescue

Mountain rescue in various parts of Scotland is maintained by the co-ordinated action of voluntary mountain-rescue teams (local climbing clubs, the police, RAF Mountain Rescue teams and other local people); also climbers in the vicinity of an accident are expected to offer their help. Official mountain-rescue posts provide a nucleus of rescue equipment for teams in the more popular climbing areas.

In the event of an accident, the quickest and simplest thing to do is contact the police (dial 999), although a local rescue post should be alerted if there is one near the vicinity of the accident.

The following are some of the mountain-rescue posts in the area through which the West Highland Way is routed, with the names of supervisors and telephone numbers.

Crianlarich Police Station	Officer in Charge 083–83–222
Glencoe Police Station	Officer in Charge 085–52–222
Fort William Police Station	Officer in Charge 0397–2361

Right of way

Under Scots law a public right of way exists when a route joins two public places or places of public resort, and when the route has been used by members of the public without let or hindrance over the prescriptive period of twenty years. Over the past 125 years, the Scottish Rights of Way Society has done much to preserve for the public the old tracks and drove-roads which lead the walker through some of the finest parts of the Scottish countryside.

With the passing of the Countryside (Scotland) Act 1967, a duty has been placed on local planning authorities to preserve and protect and keep free from obstruction all rights of way in their areas. Effectively to carry out this duty, local planning authorities have been urged to list and record rights of way, and over the past few years much progress has been made in this respect by some district councils. Much of the route of the West Highland Way lies on public rights of way and many people have walked over all or part of the route. When fully implemented, the public will have the right of passage over the whole route.

It should be understood that the public has no right to wander at large over private ground and a person who does so is a trespasser. A trespasser cannot be prosecuted for trespassing unless the proprietor can show that damage has been caused, but the proprietor or his agent can ask the person to leave his land by a specific route. Generally the attitude of landowners to the genuine walker is not an unfriendly one, provided that the latter shows reasonable thought for sporting and agricultural interests and strictly adheres to the Countryside Code (see page 21).

The Scottish Rights of Way Society continues to do valuable work in advising local planning authorities; and any reader interested in further information about the law of right of way in Scotland, or in joining the Society, should write to the Honorary Secretary, 28 Rutland Square, Edinburgh EH1 2BW.

Hill-walking and proprietary rights

It is essential to consider and respect proprietary and sporting rights; during the lambing season, for example, care must be taken to avoid disturbing ewes and lambs in sheep-rearing areas. Climbers and hill-walkers who wish to go to the hills from the beginning of

August to mid-October should first, if possible, obtain the consent of the local stalkers or game-keepers. On most estates no attempt is made to restrict access by walkers or climbers, except when stalking is in progress.

Country Code
All users of the countryside should observe the Country Code which is as follows:

1 Guard against all risks of fire
2 Fasten all gates
3 Keep dogs under proper control
4 Keep to paths across farmland
5 Avoid damaging fences, hedges and walls
6 Leave no litter
7 Safeguard water supplies
8 Protect wild life, wild plants and trees
9 Go carefully on country roads
10 Respect the life of the countryside

Milngavie at present is the official southern starting-point of the
West Highland Way and this chapter can be omitted by the walker
who prefers to be clear of towns as quickly as possible. However,
for the purist, the start can be made within the city – something that
is unique as far as long-distance walking routes are concerned. The
city of Glasgow is well endowed with public parks and the concept
of linking town and country by means of walkways through these
parks is well demonstrated by the now-established Kelvin Walkway.
It is here the West Highland Way really begins. One approach to
the Kelvin Walkway is through the Botanic Gardens.

The Botanic Gardens
Entry to the gardens is best made from the main entrance just off
Great Western Road on Queen Margaret Drive. Close at hand is
the Kibble Palace, presented by Mr John Kibble, brought from his
estate at Coulport, Loch Long, and re-erected on its present site in
1871. It was at first used for concerts and meetings, and the Earl of
Beaconsfield and Mr Gladstone delivered their rectorial addresses
under its magnificent glass dome. The façade is composed of an
entrance hall, terminated on either side by transepts, in which there
is always a beautiful display of flowers. The main feature of the
conservatory is a circular structure, 471 ft (143.6 m) in
circumference, with two domes about 40 ft (12.2 m) high. The great
tree ferns from Australia and some gigantic palms always attract
attention.
    After entering the gardens, go down a path on the right towards
the River Kelvin, cross the river by the bridge and then turn left on
to the Kelvin Walkway.
    Another approach to the Kelvin Walkway without entering the
Botanic Gardens is to cross the river by a road bridge on Queen
Margaret Drive, and turn left into Kelvin Drive where there are
entries on the left into the Kelvin Walkway.

Kelvin Walkway
Lyle's immortal song, 'Let us haste to Kelvin Grove, bonnie lassie
O', must have been inspired by the beauty of the River Kelvin with
its wooded banks and grassy slopes. Follow the path on the right

(east) bank of the River Kelvin: the route goes under several bridges including the beautiful Kirklee Bridge.

The Kelvin Walkway was opened on 10 September 1970 – European Conservation Year – by Councillor W. Marshall Hutcheson, then convenor of Glasgow Corporation Parks Committee, I always feel a little nostalgic as I walk this stretch and remember the opening ceremony. Four companions and I walked from Fort William in four days, to arrive at the ceremony with a sealed message of congratulation from the Provost of Fort William (Canon G.K.B. Henderson) and to gain a little publicity for the then Highland Way.

After about $\frac{1}{2}$ mile (0.81 kms) the high flats of Wyndford can be seen on the right; these are built on the site of the Maryhill Barracks – once a well known Glasgow landmark but now demolished to make way for this modern housing estate. When the path emerges on to a motor road, cross and turn left at St Gregory's church. Continue on the pavement for about 30 yds (27.5 m), picking up the path again on the right. Ahead is the first glimpse of the Campsie Fells. Keeping the river on the left, the walkway passes under a bridge and soon reaches another road; cross the Kelvin by the bridge on the left, and the path continues on the other side of the river.

Dawsholm Park

Leave the river by the path which rises up some steps as the route enters Dawsholm Park. At the top of the steps keep to the right-hand path above the river; by following the yellow markers of Dawsholm Nature Trail you will come to a main path, which leads down to park gates at Ilay Road. A bird sanctuary is a special feature in this park.

After leaving Dawsholm Park, a spell of walking on busy roads is unavoidable before reaching Milngavie, as further stretches of walkway need to be undertaken before the walker is free of traffic. A short stretch down Ilay Road is the main Bearsden Road. Turn right on this and continue until you reach the large roundabout at Canniesburn Toll. Take the centre road ahead for 2 miles (3.22 kms) to Milngavie.

The Antonine Wall

Although road-walking is unpleasant with the noise and smell of vehicles, there is a very interesting diversion about 1 mile (1.61 kms) north of Canniesburn Toll. The road crosses the line of the Roman Wall of Antoninus Pius, which extended from the Forth to the Clyde. This was for about fifty years the most north-westerly frontier of the Roman Empire. During that period the Wall served as a base for military operations into enemy territory, with a line of outposts running to the edge of the Scottish Highlands.

Look out for Boclair Road which runs off the main road to the right. At the road junction a little plaque on the wall states 'Roman Wall Section – 800 yards on left in cemetery'. If this interests you, go along Boclair Road to the New Kilpatrick cemetery, where two well-preserved stretches of the stone base of the Wall are exposed to view. From the cemetery westwards to Bearsden, there are no remains of the Antonine frontier to be seen, although a modern road – Roman Road – almost certainly runs above the Military Road at least for part of its length.

What is now known as the Antonine Wall was a triple formation; it consisted of a Ditch about 30 ft (9.14 m) wide and 12 ft (3.66 m) deep; a Vallum or rampart of turf south of that, at a distance which varies from 20 to 120 ft (6 to 36.6 m), raised upon a foundation of stone 14 ft (4 m) wide; and south of that again, a Military Road which the other two items were probably chiefly designed to protect.

The Hadrian and Antonine Walls are often popularly compared with the Great Wall of China, but not only is the latter a structure far more massive and extensive than anything the Romans ever attempted in the way of ramparts, it was also erected for a different purpose – as an impassable barrier against barbaric invaders. The Antonine Wall, on the other hand, was nothing more than a line of delimitation, the north-west boundary mark of Roman rule.

Those interested in Roman antiquities in Scotland, especially the Antonine Wall, would do well to read the small booklet *The Antonine Wall* by Anne S. Robertson, published by the Glasgow Archaeological Society.

The Bennie Railplane

From Boclair Road continue on the main road past Hillfoot Railway Station. On the right-hand side of the road as you approach Milngavie, there was a landmark well known to an older generation of Glaswegians – Bennie's Railplane. Unfortunately it was removed in 1956 and one cannot now see this eye-catching creation which was rather like something from the works of Jules Verne or H.G. Wells.

George Bennie was born in 1892 and he proposed lifting the railways off the ground: he envisaged a 'rail' suspended in the air, along with a streamlined 'plane' with its own motive power – electric or internal combustion – would travel at over 100 m.p.h. (161 k.p.h.). The track itself was not very exciting but the 'car' suspended from the top frame was cigar-shaped, with four-bladed propellors at either end – a spectacularly aerodynamic vehicle long before the word had come into use. It was built by the Scottish firm William Beardmore & Company, who also built another famous cigar-shaped object – the airship, R-34.

Early in 1930, as the Bennie Railpane travelled to and fro along the experimental length of track, Bennie sought encouragement from the railway companies. But although at the beginning they showed interest, they cooled off as the effects of the Depression were felt. He never found a customer and died at Epsom in 1957, a bitterly disappointed man. As an exercise in engineering, the Bennie Railplane was a perfectly workable proposition, and the monorail system is being adopted in other countries. Unfortunately George Bennie was born a little before his time.

Milngavie

Milngavie is now a dormitory town of Glasgow and there is sadly little historical documentation of the burgh and surrounding area. As a place-name 'Milguy' is quite old; it appears as such in Timothy Pont's *Picture of Scotland*, issued in 1654 from Amsterdam. Those wishing to start the West Highland Way from Milngavie can easily reach the town from Glasgow by train (Sunday excepted) or bus.

Accommodation
The West End of Glasgow has many hotels which are near the
Kelvin Walkway. The Glasgow Youth Hostel at 10 Woodlands
Terrace is also close to this starting-point. There is a hotel in
Milngavie for those wishing to stay there.

Suggestion for an additional walk in this section
Milngavie to the Auld Wives Lifts and back – 6 miles (9.66 kms)
From Milngavie railway station walk along Station Road and cross
the main Glasgow road. Continue along Baldernock Road for about
1 mile (1.61 kms) until you reach Baldernock Church. The country
road to the right a little past the church takes you to the farm of
High Blochairn: from there go right uphill by the cart road to North
Blochairn. Now you are on the edge of the Moor of Craigmaddie,
across which there is a track to the famous Auld Wives Lifts. It is as
well to ask permission at North Blochairn to cross the moor as this is
private ground.

   The remarkable group of enormous, naturally poised blocks of
sandstone occupies the centre of a large circular hollow near the
middle of the rocky moor. The top or table stone measures 22 ft by
11 ft (6.7 m by 3.4 m) and the two supporting blocks are respectively
20 ft by 8 ft (6 m by 2.5 m) and 14 ft by 10 ft (4.3 m by 3.0 m).
Strange legends cling around these huge stones.

   The folklore is that the structure was formed by the united
exertions of three old women or witches. These weird sisters
engaged in a trial of strength, in which victory was to go to the one
who should carry a large stone the greatest distance. One took up
her 'lift' and carried it along until she dropped it at this place. The
second lifted her ponderous burden and carried it forward, but by
mischance let it fall close to that of the first. Seeing this, the third
raised a larger stone than the other two and, to show her
superiority, hurled it with ease on top of the two preceding stones.

   A more prosaic geological theory of its origin is that these
boulders were erratics left during a phase of the Ice Age.

   On the nearly level surface of the highest stone is a curious
archaeological feature. This is an incised ring with a diameter of 36
ins (0.91 m), bearing every appearance of having been carved at

some very remote period. The stones have been claimed as a Druidical altar and the incised ring is mentioned as 'the ancient sanctifying emblem'. The old spelling of the moor's name was Craig-madden. Madden has been translated as *moidhean*, meaning entreaty, supplication; so – the rock of prayer.

While doing field-work for this book, I visited the Auld Wives Lifts and I met a gentleman who became interested in my clambering on top of them. He asked me what I was looking for and I said that I was looking for cup and ring marks, but could find none. After I had scrambled down, he asked me to take a closer look at some of the corners of the stones and see if I could see faces. At first I could not, but then he showed me where to look and several carved faces began to stare out at me. Although I have visited the Auld Wives Lifts on several occasions, this was a feature new to me. The carvings seem very old, and could date back to the ancient Celts, who carved stone heads.

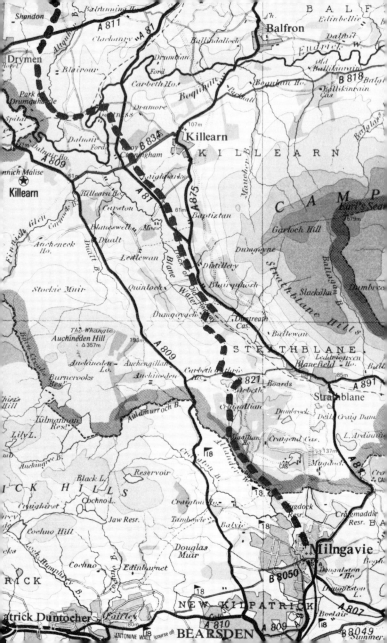

The town of Milngavie gives quick access to the West Highland
Way. Leave Douglas Street opposite the War Memorial and walk
down a lane between two rows of shops at a bridge over the
Allander Water. Cross the road and take the tarmac path by the
edge of a small housing estate. Continue along a tree-lined track,
which was once an old railway line, for approximately $\frac{1}{4}$ mile (0.4
kms); turn left and then right, following the signposts to pick up the
path by the Allander Water.

The Allander Park
The path follows the east bank of the stream through the pleasant
Allander Park for a $\frac{1}{4}$ mile (0.4 kms) before striking uphill to the
right. The Way continues in a north-westerly direction through the
outer fringe of Mugdock Wood. At the end of the wood is a motor
road. Turn left for about 30 yds (27.43 m), and where the road
sweeps left on a sharp bend, turn right through a small wooden
gate. Follow a grassy path high above the river: in wet weather parts
of this path can be very boggy.

Mugdock Castle
This ruined castle built in the fourteenth century lies north-east of
the West Highland Way behind Mugdock Wood. The structure has
been much altered over the centuries and little is known about its
history. The only events recorded are that the castle and barony
were acquired from Maldwin, Earl of Lennox, in the reign of
Alexander II, by David de Grahame, in exchange for certain lands
in Galloway. In 1646 the castle became the principal residence of
the Montrose family, whose name is honourably distinguished in
the history of Scotland, but tradition is silent about their association
with it. In 1875 John Guthrie built a mansion on the ruins of the old
castle.

Highland Gateway
Proposals to develop this area were the subject of a local public
enquiry in July 1971; these included plans for hotel, sport, trade and
conference facilities including restaurants, a cinema/theatre, a
night-club, a golf club, a nature reserve, an angling loch,

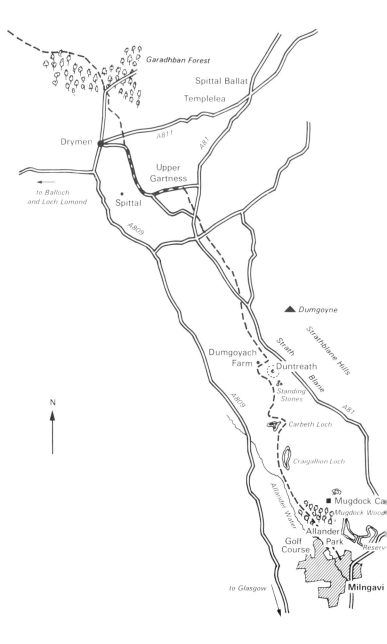

illuminated gardens, an area of residential development and the restoration of Mugdock Castle. The entire complex was to be called 'Highland Gateway'; however the scheme has fallen through owing to the lack of financial support.

Craigallian

The path continues along the west side of Craigallian Loch and later skirts the east side of Carbeth Loch; the route is now following an old stage-coach road. Wooden holiday chalets are scattered on the land in this area.

Where the path comes out on to the motor road (B821), turn left and walk about a $\frac{1}{4}$ mile (0.4 kms) along the road, then pick up the path on the right and proceed northwards past the farm Arlehaven. Now there are extensive views over the Blane Valley, dominated on the right by the Strathblane Hills with the extinct volcano, Dumgoyne, at the extreme end. Ben Lomond can be seen in the far distance. The path swings round Duntreath Hill and comes out at Dumgoyach Farm; continue a short distance down the farm road and cross the bridge over the Blane Water. Turn left immediately and continue on the disused line of the Aberfoyle/Blanefield railway.

Standing Stones – Dumgoyach

The Standing Stones at Dumgoyach were scheduled as an Ancient Monument in 1963; they consist of five stones running in a straight line from south-west to north-east. The two stones at the south-west end and one at the north-east are still upright, while the other two are lying on the ground. Single standing stones may be marks of graves but arrangement in groups could indicate their use in religious rites. No tradition, however, has reached modern times as to what the Dumgoyach Stones might have represented.

Duntreath

The castle, rebuilt in the nineteenth century, has been owned by the Edmonstone family since the fifteenth century. It cannot be seen from the route of the West Highland Way.

The Blane Valley

The route for the West Highland Way follows the disused railway line, part of which is now owned by the Central Scotland Water Development Board. A large pipe takes water from Loch Lomond; where it is above ground, it is disguised by an earth embankment. The old railway line crosses the main motor road (A81) at the Beech Tree Inn on the site of a former station. Soon the dilapidated buildings of the former Killearn Hospital come into view on the left. At one time proposals were considered for developing the area as a recreational reception centre and caravan site, but to date the buildings remain derelict.

Along the pipe-line the Water Board have installed padlocked gates at road crossings. Stiles are provided to facilitate access, and although the Water Board does not discourage walkers, it is in the interests of users to observe the Country Code. Although views are very restricted in this section, bird-life is quite prolific and it is a good area to watch out for pheasants.

The route continues under the B834 road, and after $\frac{1}{2}$ mile (0.8 kms) again crosses the A81 and runs along the old railway track for a further $\frac{1}{2}$ mile (0.8 kms). The Way then leaves the track of the old railway and continues on the minor road from Killearn to Drymen by Gartness.

Gartness

This is a pleasant little hamlet which attracts many visitors in the autumn when salmon come up the Endrick to spawn. Nothing remains now of Gartness Castle on the right-hand bank of the Endrick Water south of Gartness Bridge, but this was at one time the home of John Napier (1550–1617), inventor of logarithms. His forebears – the Napiers of Merchiston – owned land here, and he spent various periods of his life in the district. Stones from the castle are believed to have been used to build Gartness Mill, now a ruin but which still has date stones inscribed 1574 and 1689.

By following the little road which climbs steeply at first to Upper Gartness, fine views are obtained looking back to Dumgoyne and the Campsie Hills. Continue on this minor road, first westwards and then northwards towards Drymen: it is here that the walker obtains

his first view of Loch Lomond. Where the minor road turns
westward at Gateside, the Way follows an old right-of-way path
northwards across an open field to the A811 road opposite Drymen
Primary School. It is only a short distance westwards at this point
for those wishing to visit Drymen.

Temples and Spittals
This section is of interest to the historian and the student of place-
names, since 'temple' and 'spittal' appear on maps of the area.
During the Crusades, certain military orders were founded to give
protection to the pilgrims who journeyed to the Holy Land. The
principal orders were the Knights of the Temple (at Jerusalem),
better known as the Knights Templars, and the Knights St John of
Jerusalem or Knights Hospitallers. Many wealthy people joined,
and often made grants of land to their Orders; these domains, in
Scotland, became known as Temple or Spittal lands. The Order of
Knights of the Temple was suppressed by the Pope in 1312 and their
lands were transferred to the Knights Hospitallers, so the name
Spittal is more common than Temple.

   Examples of these names still surviving are Templelea and Spittal
Ballat near the junction of the motor roads A811 and A81, $3\frac{1}{4}$ miles
(5.23 kms) east of Drymen; the name Spittal occurs again near
Croftamie School about 2 miles (3.22 kms) south of Drymen. There
is a district in the west side of Glasgow still called 'Temple' derived
from the lands of the Templars; after the First World War, Glasgow
Corporation built a large housing suburb on part of this ground
which is appropriately called 'Knightswood'.

Accommodation
There are two comfortable hotels in Drymen and a few houses in
the village take people for bed and breakfast, but it is recommended
to book accommodation in advance.

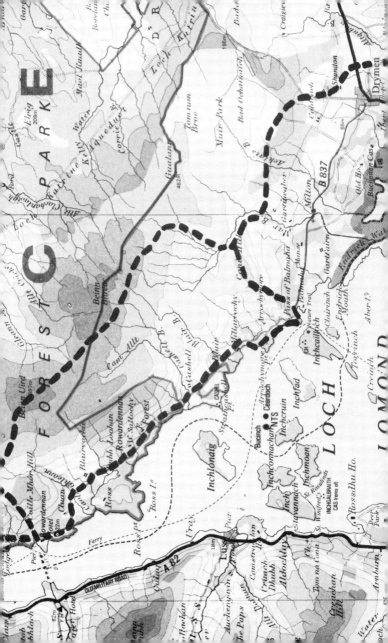

From Drymen, to rejoin the West Highland Way head in an easterly direction along the A811 for about 1 mile (1.61 kms), then strike north opposite Blarnavaid farm and continue by farm- and forest-track through Garadhban Forest.

Garadhban Forest
This area is under the management of the Forestry Commission and there is a wide variety of larch and spruce trees. To encourage walkers to use the area, the Commission has provided a number of footpaths, making walking comparatively pleasant with excellent views of Loch Lomond and surrounding countryside. No doubt, however, as the trees mature, these fine views will be restricted.

The West Highland Way keeps in the direction of Conic Hill which is easily seen from the main path; the route crosses a narrow road leading to Moorpark and continues northwards to end just short of the Commission's fence at the north-west corner of Garadhban Forest; a stile has now been erected at that north-west corner of the forest.

Burn of Mar
Once over the stile follow the signposts and cross the newly erected bridge over the Kilandan Blandan Burn. Another bridge, over the Burn of Mar, takes the walker on to the base of Conic Hill.

The Countryside Commission's original proposal for the West Highland Way in this area was a high-level route which was also recommended by the outdoor organisations, but after consultation with the local authorities and the Forestry Commission a lower route was selected. It was recognised, however, that it would be desirable to develop a higher alternative route at a later date. The two routes separate at the base of Conic Hill on the course of the Burn of Mar.

Official Route via Conic Hill to Balmaha
Leave the Burn of Mar and ascend the shoulder of Conic Hill; the climb is reasonably straightforward but the marker posts at certain times of the year may be difficult to locate, owing to high bracken. The view from the summit is exceptional as it is on the Highland

Boundary Fault; the division of highland and lowland scenery by
the Highland Line is clearly seen across Loch Lomond with its
islands and the hills beyond. Descend from the ridge of Conic Hill
through a gap to the south-east, then go westwards on a deep
bracken path which eventually links up with a forest walk leading to
the public car-park at Balmaha.

Balmaha to Rowardennan

From the car park at Balmaha, cross the motor road and join the
board walk round the head of the bay. The motor road turns steeply
uphill through the Pass of Balmaha, but the Way continues for a few
yards along the old road towards the pier before it too climbs
steeply up to the right, to a vantage-point; here an indicator
commemorates the opening of the West Highland Way by the Earl
of Mansfield. Splendid views of Loch Lomond, its islands, and the
surrounding hills, are obtained from this point.

From the cairn continue a few yards along the hill top, then drop
sharply down through the oakwoods to the shore. The Way then
meanders along the loch-side through woods adjoining boating and
car-park areas. When Milarrochy Bay is reached, the Way
continues on the motor road before joining a track on the right-
hand verge at Milarrochy Cottage; after a short distance the route
recrosses the road at the Blair Burn, and enters the Queen
Elizabeth Forest Park. The path keeps close to the road, crosses a
small plank bridge to come out at an open field. The Way then
strikes through a very dark coniferous forest, which later becomes
more open with deciduous trees, and finally a gentle descent brings
the walker out at Cashell Farm road end.

The West Highland Way follows the road on the long straight
stretch, then takes to a path on the verge as far as Anchorage
Cottage. From here the route goes out to the road again to
Sallochy, where it turns left towards the loch amidst oakwoods.
After a short distance by the shore, the route turns inland and
climbs over a ridge, then drops down to the north-west and returns
to the shore for 2 miles (3.22 kms). The Way now passes between
the Glasgow University Field Centre at Ross, and its boat-house,
before rising steeply into Ross Wood. After almost reaching the

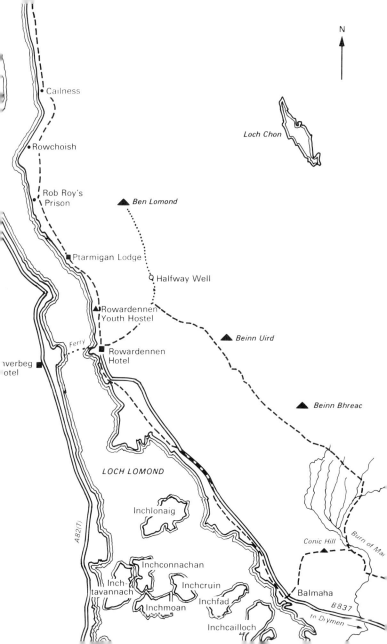

summit above the loch, the route descends gradually for $\frac{1}{2}$ mile (0.8 kms) to reach open ground and then continues through woodland on the left until it reaches the cottage at Coille Mhor. The route crosses a burn and climbs over a hillock in a dark larch plantation before it returns to the loch shore in an oakwood. After a few hundred yards it goes inland again and joins the motor road about $\frac{1}{4}$ mile (0.4 kms) from the Rowardennan Hotel.

Alternative High-Level Route

In the words of the famous song I would suggest 'You tak' the High Road'. In order to see Loch Lomond and its islands to the best possible advantage, the high-level alternative is better.

Follow the Burn of Mar up the west bank and after passing the base of Conic Hill, ascend along any of the Burn's tributaries to reach higher and drier ground – the low-lying area stretching north-west from the foot of Conic Hill can be very wet. After climbing for about 1 mile (1.61 kms) strike north-west and contour round Beinn Bhreac; this entails approximately 3 miles (4.83 kms) of rough walking but good views are opening up now and are ample reward for the effort.

It is worth an extra little climb to head in a northerly direction and continue to the summit of Beinn Uird (1,957 ft–596.2 m). The views here are magnificent and provide a dramatic introduction to the Highland scenery which will accompany the walker for many miles now. Ben Lomond in front predominates but other giants are beginning to appear to the north-west across Loch Lomond; in contrast to the wild grandeur which is unfolding, the islands lie peacefully on the loch against a background of gentle lowland country. Loch Lomond is one of Scotland's most beautiful lochs, and apart from the view gained by sailing on it, one can only appreciate its beauty fully by seeing it from such a high vantage-point.

Leaving Beinn Uird, continue north-west in the direction of Ben Lomond and then swing gradually west in a gentle curve towards the lower slopes of the Ben. The main Ben Lomond path will be

Loch Lomond – Ben Vorlich centre background

seen ahead: join this for the final descent to Rowardennan.

Since this alternative high-level route is not official there is no track, nor any West Highland Way signposts. The terrain consists mostly of heather which makes the going rough, and there are pot-holes which can be dangerous, especially in snow conditions.

Loch Lomond

On a fine day the sailing-trip up Loch Lomond from Balloch is one of the most delightful in the world. The *Countess Fiona* operates from the beginning of April to the end of September. It is advisable to check dates and times beforehand, and information may be obtained from Ind Coope Alloa Brewery Co Ltd, Anderston House, 389 Argyle Street, Glasgow; tel: 041–226–4271.

The Loch is $22\frac{1}{2}$ miles (36.2 kms) long and at its widest near the southern extremity is about 5 miles (8.1 kms). Its greatest depth is 623 ft (190.2 m). It is studded with thirty wooded islands of exquisite beauty and is sometimes referred to as the 'Queen of Scottish Lochs'.

The first and largest of the beautiful islands is Inch Murrin. It was used as a deer park by the Duke of Montrose and has an old ruined castle of the Earls of Lennox. After clearing Inch Murrin, you can see Rossdhu House, seat of Sir Ivor Colquhoun, Baronet of Luss, with its dark background of pine-clad hills. The next islets are Creinch and Torrinch, and on the eastern shore on a headland is Ross Priory, where Sir Walter Scott stayed while gathering information for *Rob Roy*. The next large island is Inch Cailleach, or 'Women's Island', so named because a nunnery once existed there; its cemetery was a burial place of the MacGregors.

Several other islands lie to the west of Inch Cailleach, the chief of these being Inch Fad – the long island – partly under cultivation; Inch Moan – the peat island – very low-lying; Inch Tavannach – Monk's Island; Inch Connachan – Colquhoun's Island; Inch Cruin, arable and cultivated; Inch Lonaig, occupied as a deer park and remarkable for its fine yew trees. On Inch Galbraith, a small island a little south of Inch Tavannach, there are the ruins of an old castle.

Accommodation
There is a hotel at Rowardennan, which is open from April to
October; the youth hostel is open from the last week in February
until the end of October.

Rowardennan to Inversnaid 7.5 miles (12.07 kms)

A little beyond Rowardennan Hotel, the motor road ends at the car-park near the pier. Behind the car-park, the route at first follows the Forestry Commission's track to Inversnaid. Soon Rowardennan Youth Hostel is reached on the left, and a little further on the scattered houses of Ardess can be seen. The track, which is in good condition, is now rising steadily, and after $\frac{1}{2}$ mile (0.8 kms) Ptarmigan Lodge can be seen on the left. Continue for a few hundred yards and leave the Forestry track as the Way drops down sharply to the left, to follow the shore.

The walking on this stretch is very pleasant, mainly through oak and birch woodland, although at times it may be steep above the loch. After approximately 2 miles (3.22 kms) there is a recess in one of the grey cliffs overlooking the loch, known as Rob Roy's Prison; here he is supposed to have kept his captives. If they proved recalcitrant, he had them lowered into the loch at the end of a rope – or so the story goes.

Beyond Rob Roy's Prison the Way continues along the shore and joins a spur track from the forest road above. On this stretch there are fine views opposite of the Arrochar Alps including 'The Cobbler'. Continue uphill through coniferous woodland for $\frac{1}{2}$ mile (0.8 kms) to Rowchoish. The 'William Ferris Memorial Shelter' known as Rowchoish Bothy is off the path on the left and although hidden among the trees it is well signposted. It was provided jointly by the Forestry Commission and the Scottish Rights of Way Society. William Ferris was a past president of the Federation of Scottish Ramblers and would have welcomed the concept of the West Highland Way. One wall of the bothy is exposed to the elements, and it is built up only half-way on two sides, but it would serve as an overnight shelter in an emergency. It is under the care of the Mountain Bothies Association.

From Rowchoish the route rises through woodland to rejoin the forest track, which terminates after a few hundred yards; however the Way continues by a pleasant woodland path to the Cailness Burn. A little further on Cailness cottage can be seen on the right.

Rowardennan Hotel

Rob Roy's Cave

Inveruglas I.

Wallace's I.

Inversnaid Hotel

Ferry   Pier   Falls

Garrison   Glen   Arklet

Corriearklet

Loch Arklet

Corriehichon

Kenmore Wood

Cruinalan
△537m
L. Cruachain

Beinn Vanaho

Elarannich

Gleann Gaoithe

Cruach Tairbeirt
△415m

Inbhir a' Chaillinn

Culness

Cailness B.

Craim a' Bheinn

Tarbet I.

Tarbet

Pier

Creag a' Bhocain

Doram Achaidh B.

Cotner

Beinn Dubh

Stuckivoulich

Rob Roy's Prison

QUEEN
ELIZABETH
BEN LOMOND
(3192ft) △974m
FOREST PARK

L. Dubh

Stuckgown Ho.

Ben Reoch

R. Ban

Rubha Dubh

Beinn a' Bhan

Firkin

Ptarmigan Lo.

BUCHANAN
ELIZABETH

Bruach Caore

Beinn Bhreac

Rubha Mor

Moire Eich

Dun

Camas-nan Clais

Rowardennan Lodge

Ardess

Elrig

Invergroin

Stob Gobhlach

Pier

Caille Mhor Hill

Rowardennan Hotel

Beinn Uird
△597m

FORE

Doune

Douglas Water Hotel

82m

Cluan

Caol Ghleann

Doune

Blairvockie

Mid Hill

Glen Dubh

Beinn Dubh

Ross

Dubh Lochan

Rowardennan
W. Sallochy
Forest

Ross Pt.

Glen Mollochan

Ross I.

Eich

Oulag

Edentaggart

Glennacloichan

Uray

Inchlonaig

CASHEL

Glen   Luss   Water

Auchengavin

Luss   Pier

18m

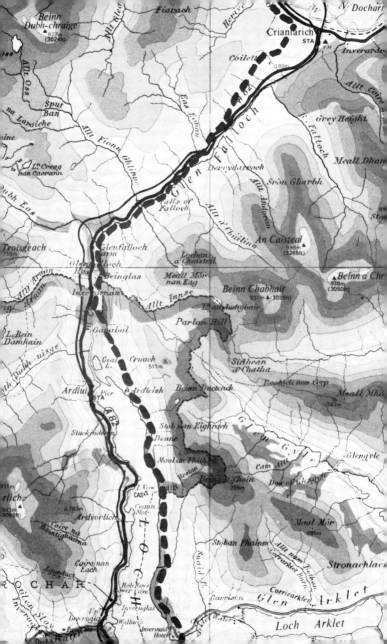

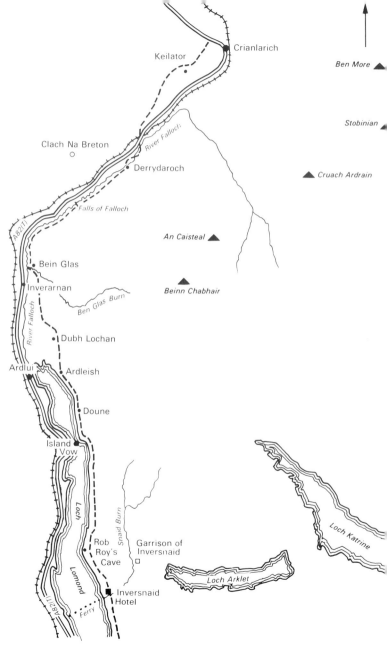

This is a delightful walk at any time of the year but particularly during the autumn when the red and gold of the tree-colourings blend with the rich orange and brown of the bracken on the hillsides. Another 2 miles (3.22 kms) brings you to the bridge over the Snaid Burn and so to Inversnaid, where there is a comfortable hotel open throughout the year.

Craigroyston

This is the Craigroyston area: Crag Rostan or Craig Royston was a small estate which at one time was owned by the famous (or infamous) character, Rob Roy. It extended down the eastern shores of Loch Lomond from the mouth of Glen Falloch to the base of Ben Lomond.

The Craig Royston story goes further back in history, however, and the First Statistical Account contains this entry:

'In Craigrostan there are several caves . . . one commonly known by the name of King Robert's (Robert the Bruce) cave . . . The report is, that the night in which King Robert slept in the cave, he was surrounded with wild goats that used to lie there in the night, and when he arose in the morning, and found himself so comfortable, he was so well pleased with the goats as his bedfellows, that, when he came to be king, he made a law that all goats should be grass mail (or grass rent) free.'

The Craigroyston goats are impressive beasts, ranging in colour from black to nearly white, with massive horns. They are shy, but the walker may be rewarded by seeing some in the woods near Cailness if he moves along the track noiselessly.

Although this area is no great distance from Glasgow the golden eagle still breeds here in the upper heights, and the peregrine and the raven remain in their ancestral haunts. The wildcat – a most elusive creature in the Highlands – has been reported as far south in Scotland as this district.

The Craigroyston Pump-Storage Scheme

The North of Scotland Hydro-Electricity Board plans to construct a pump-storage power scheme in the Craigroyston zone. The scheme envisages the creation of a storage lake at about 1,575 ft (480 m) between Ben Lomond and Creag a' Bhocain, retained on the north-west by a soil dam some 200 ft (60 m) high. The feed-outs from the dam together with the scheme's turbines and powerhouse will be underground and access to them will be along the forest road which will need to be upgraded to a point about 0.6 miles (1 km) south of Rowchoish, from where it will approach the powerhouse itself by underground road. The Loch Lomond outfall and intake for the scheme will be well below water level and thus not visible.

In order to construct this scheme, which will be one of the biggest undertaken in Europe, new roads will have to be constructed to transport men and materials to the site. The effects of this will change the entire east bank of Loch Lomond as far as Rowchoish. The threat will be greater once the roads are built and the work completed, because pressure from the motoring public may force the Hydro Board to open up the roads to the public at large.

The Loch Lomond area is a very sensitive one, being the last remaining wilderness zone of countryside near Glasgow. The route of the West Highland Way would have to be changed, but this is only one small price which future generations would have to pay if the bonnie banks of Loch Lomond disappeared. At Inversnaid one can look across at the power station at Loch Sloy and see the ugly pipes which ruin the west bank of the Loch: now the east side of the Loch is also under threat. This scheme, however, has been suspended meantime.

Inversnaid
The waterfall at the bridge over the Snaid Burn is very impressive and when admiring the waterfall it may interest the onlooker to learn that William Wordsworth also stood near here and found inspiration for his celebrated poem, 'To a Highland Girl':

> Nor am I loath, though pleased at heart,
> Sweet Highland girl! from thee to part;
> For I, methinks, till I grow old,
> As fair before me shall behold,

Rowardennan Youth Hostel, with the lower slope of Ben Lomond

As I do now, the cabin small,
The lake, the bay, the waterfall;
And thee, the spirit of them all!

About 1 mile (1.6 kms) east of Inversnaid Hotel stands the old
garrison of Inversnaid; all that remains is now incorporated into
farm buildings. It was established here in 1713 to keep Rob Roy and
his clan in check. General Wolfe of Quebec served here as a young
officer.

The literary and historical scene around Inversnaid would not be
complete without reference to Sir Walter Scott and his famous
character – Rob Roy.

Rob Roy
Scott's book *Rob Roy* was based on the real man who was the Robin
Hood of Scotland. A kinsman of the chief of the MacGregors, he is
the legendary hero of this district. Rob Roy spent his early years in
Glengyle and his last years in Balquhidder, but Inversnaid with its
crags and forests was his own particular domain.

His speculations as a cattle dealer failed and in 1712 the Duke of
Montrose seized his estates as security for unpaid debts. He had to
withdraw to Breadalbane to escape his creditors, and in his absence
the Duke's agent brutally evicted his wife and children. Rob
returned to Craig Royston after the 1715 Jacobite rebellion, and
lived openly among his kinsmen under the protection of Montrose's
powerful rival, the Duke of Argyll.

The following story is typical of the man: One day in the year
1716 when on his way from Inversnaid to Aberfoyle in the
Trossachs, he was told of the plight of a widow on the Duke of
Montrose's estate. She was in arrears with the rent of her small
farm, and the estate factor was about to sell her belongings in lieu of
the overdue rent. Rob Roy immediately decided to help her. He
called on the widow and advanced her the sum of money she was
due, his one stipulation being that she was to obtain a written
receipt from the factor for the money. Then Roy Roy with some of
his men went to an inn nearby, where he knew that the factor was
likely to call on his way home.

The factor duly arrived and after his glass of whisky he departed in a happy frame of mind. Rob Roy and his men sprang out and seized him, taking the money which the widow had paid. So Rob regained the money and had the added excitement of the adventure. The widow was able to show a written receipt for her rent and could not be called on to pay further rent that year.

After his many adventures, it is remarkable that Rob Roy had the good fortune to die from natural causes in his own bed. The following intimation of his death appeared in the *Courant and Mercury*:

On Saturday was se'n night (Dec. 28, 1734) died at Balquhidder, in Perthshire, the famous Highland partisan, Rob Roy.

Inversnaid to Inverarnan 6.5 miles (10.5 kms)
Leaving Inversnaid Hotel a path runs north along the east bank of Loch Lomond to Rob Roy's Cave – a natural cavern near the water's edge at the foot of a precipitous cliff. This is sometimes known as Bruce's Cave, as tradition has it that this was the cave where Robert the Bruce sheltered after the Battle of Dail Righ in 1306, under the protection of a MacGregor chief.

Considerable care must be taken here and for the next few miles as this section is the roughest of the whole route, and extra time should be allowed. The Way clambers up and down from the loch shore and there is a fair amount of scrambling over and around fallen rocks and trees. Although it may be rough, conditions have improved considerably since the first surveys were made in the late Sixties – at that time it was an impenetrable jungle. The authorities are to be congratulated for the manner in which this stretch of the route has been cleared and made easier for the walker.

Island of I Vow
From certain stretches of the rough passage between Rob Roy's Cave and Doune (if you are on the shore) an island can be observed on the Loch. This is the island of I Vow. The ruined castle on it was built in 1577 and was apparently used by the MacFarlanes when Cromwell destroyed their castle at Inveruglas. The name means 'the

island of stores', and as it lies midway between the lands of the
MacFarlanes (west bank) and the MacGregors (east bank), it was
probably a place where the clans interchanged their spoils by barter.

Another theory about the ruin on the island is that it was a former
priory, and in support of this theory a curious argument is brought
forward. On the little island there grows, in luxuriant profusion, the
daffodil, a flower found nowhere else growing wild in the district. It
is pointed out that wherever the daffodil flourishes in those
Highland solitudes, it always is found that there has been some
former religious settlement – the flower having been cultivated for
special use at Easter and other festivals of the Church.

Beinglas and Inveraran

On reaching the ruined cottage of Doune, walking conditions
become easier; the route returns to the loch shore and soon
Ardleish comes into view, in just over 1 mile (1.61 kms). After
leaving the old farm of Ardleish, cross the burn and climb up by an
old path which continues behind Cnap Mor and on to Dubh Lochan
(the black loch). At the top of the pass one obtains good views of
the Ben Lui group to the north. The path retains its height for a few
hundred yards before dropping down through woods to Glen
Falloch. Cross the bridge over the Ben Glas Burn which,
incidentally, marks the boundary line between Strathclyde and
Central Regions.

Above Ben Glas Burn is a spectacular series of waterfalls which
unfortunately cannot be seen to advantage from the route. If the
walker, however, wishes to visit the Inverarnan Hotel, there is an
access path from the burn to the A82 road where a fine view of the
falls is obtained. The Inverarnan Hotel is open all year.

The West Highland Way is routed behind Beinglas Farm and
follows a 'dry-stane dyke' northwards. Although the views are
restricted, it is a very pleasant woodland walk, and a little more
than $\frac{1}{2}$ mile (0.8 kms) beyond the farm, the Way crosses a stile by a
sheep fank. From here on it follows a rough track through Glen
Falloch. Splendid views can be obtained of the River Falloch and its
succession of gorges, waterfalls, and pools. The Falls of Falloch are
a well-known local attraction, especially when the river is in spate.

Clach-na-Breton

The Way continues to rise through open moorland, and it is from hereabouts, not very far beyond the Falls of Falloch on the lower slopes of Cruachan Cruinn on the other side of the main road (A82), that you may glimpse a very interesting boulder known as the Clach-na-Breton. The boulder is of a peculiar formation and stands out like a cannon. It was here that Robert the Bruce paused to reconnoitre after his defeat by the MacDougalls of Lorn at the Battle of Dail Righ. When he reached the 'Mortar Stone' he stopped to see whether immediate pursuit had been shaken off. He was on his way to the fastnesses of Loch Lomond where, as already stated in this chapter, he found shelter in a cave at Craig Royston.

Near this stone there used to be an old highland *clachan* (hamlet) from which the stone took its Gaelic name. When the engineers were cutting the line for the West Highland railway they found remains of furnaces for smelting iron.

According to William F. Skene in his famous work, *Celtic Scotland*, the importance of the Clach-na-Breton goes further back in history because it formed a natural boundary marker for three ancient kingdoms – the boundaries of Strathclyde, Dalriada and Pictland met at this point above Loch Lomond.

Derrydaroch

Glen Falloch begins to open up a little and you can see scattered Scots pines on the east side of the glen – gnarled remnants of the old Caledonian Forest. The route crosses the Falloch at the Derrydaroch bridge and turns sharp right over a hillock in a birchwood. Less than $\frac{1}{2}$ mile (0.8 kms) north from the bridge, the West Highland Way is routed to pass under the railway by a low, muddy, cattle creep. Cross the main road (A82) a short distance north of Carmyle Cottage, and climb uphill to join the old military road which runs alongside the electric pylons in this area.

This path follows the old Military Road built by William Caulfield, who succeeded General Wade in 1740, and although once stone-based it is now in very poor condition on this section to Crianlarich. Where bog and peat have encroached, the Countryside Commission recommended clearance, and drainage will probably

be necessary as well.

Keilator Farm
After about 1 mile (1.61 kms) over this boggy section, the track
keeps to the north side of a boundary wall. There are good views
over the top end of Glen Falloch, with the mountains near
Crianlarich dominating the scene to the east. The wet track skirts
Keilator Farm and here you should exercise care especially at
lambing and calving seasons. A little further on past the farm a high
stile is reached. Once over the stile the walker has a choice of
routes. This junction is well signposted. The West Highland Way
continues on a path to the left, while those wishing to visit
Crianlarich can take the track running down on the right which
eventually joins the main A82 road at a stile. Turn right for
Crianlarich.

Crianlarich
Crianlarich (Craobh an Lairige – The Tree of the Pass) is an
important centre for road and rail. The little village lies at the
junction of three valleys – Glen Dochart, Glen Falloch and Strath
Fillan. It makes an excellent walking and climbing base, handy both
for the Crianlarich hills and the Ben Lui group in the north-west.
There is a youth hostel in the village, which is open from March to
October; there is a hotel and other available accommodation,
together with restaurants and a shop.

Suggestion for an additional walk in this section
Rowardennan to Loch Ard – 9 miles (14.48 kms)
This is a popular cross-country route, directly linking Rowardennan
and Loch Ard Youth Hostels. From Rowardennan Hotel follow the
Ben Lomond path to about 1.250 ft (381 m) and then head east-by-
north to cross the Moin Eich pass and descend to the Bruach
Caoruinn burn, and so to the Duchray Water. Once in the forest,
follow a track round the west end of Loch Ard to reach Kinlochard
and Loch Ard Youth Hostel (open from the end of February to end
of October).

Cruach Ardrain from Strath Fillan

Suggestions for climbs in this section
Ben Lomond – 3,192 ft (972.9 m)
This is the most southerly of Scotland's Munros (mountains over 3,000 ft), and it is one of the most popular and frequently ascended hills in Scotland. It is very well known as Glasgow's mountain, on account of its being so near the city. The route from Rowardennan is the most popular. The path starts from the hotel and climbs north-east beside the forest; it then turns northwards to Sron Aonaich and along the crest of the broad south ridge. The path zigzags up to the summit ridge, which it follows round the corrie to the top. This path presents no difficulty in good weather, but in misty conditions care must be taken on the summit ridge. Allow about 2½ hours for the ascent.

On a clear day, a magnificent all-round panorama rewards the climber for his effort. To the west the Arrochar Alps dominate the view and possibly the 'Ben', as it is popularly called, is the best viewpoint for them. Ben Cruachan and Ben Lui are prominent to the north-west, then further round (if you are lucky enough to have good visibility) is Ben Nevis. To the north are the Crianlarich hills, and then Ben Lawers in Perthshire to the north-east. Eastwards, Stuc a'Chroin and Ben Vorlich are the principal mountains to be seen, together with the gentler Ochils beyond the wooded hills of the Trossachs. Looking south, the islands of Loch Lomond stud the water like jewels.

Beinn Chabhair – 3,053 ft (930.9 m)
The easiest starting point for Beinn Chabhair is the bridge over the River Falloch north of Inverarnan Hotel. Walk through Beinglas Farm and continue by a path which climbs beside the waterfall at the Ben Glas Burn. The path continues along the burn for about 2 miles (3.22 kms) and then reaches Lochan Beinn Chabhair. From the Lochan a steep ascent leads to the summit.

An Caisteal – 3,265 ft (994.9 m)
The usual starting point is Crianlarich, and the climber has to walk back from the village on the A82 south-westwards for about 1½ miles (2.41 kms) until a bend on the River Falloch is reached, where there

is a footbridge. Cross the bridge and proceed up the wet lower slopes of Sron Gharbh. About 200 yards (182.9 m) north of the summit is a rocky knoll with a cairn; this knoll is probably what has given the mountain its name.

Cruach Ardrain – 3,428 ft (1045.2 m)
This is a very popular mountain for climbers, particularly in winter when its impressive Y gully is filled with snow. There are extensive plantings by the Forestry Commission and the approach can be difficult. The hill-walker had best walk about ½ mile (0.81 kms) south of Crianlarich to a bridge over the railway, and climb in a southerly direction below Grey Height – this ridge provides a pleasant approach to the summit of Cruach Ardrain.

Ben More – 3,843 ft (1171.4 m) and Stobinian 3,821 ft (1165 m)
The normal way to climb Ben More is to start from Benmore Farm, which is 2 miles (3.22 kms) east of Crianlarich; climb direct up the north-west ridge. This is quite a stiff climb to the summit. A pleasanter and gentler approach starts 5 miles (8.05 kms) east of Crianlarich, and is on the north-east ridge.

  Stobinian is also climbed from Benmore Farm, following up the Benmore Burn for about 1½ miles (2.41 kms) and then turning east to ascend to the Bealach-eadar-dha-Beinn. From this col follow the north ridge of Stobinian to the summit.

  Both mountains are generally combined in the one ascent and both summits provide excellent viewpoints. On a clear day one can see almost half of Scotland, from the Cairngorms in the north to the Galloway hills in the south-west, together with both east and west coasts of Scotland.

Ben More and Stobinian from Strath Fillan (overleaf)

From Crianlarich the walker must retrace his steps to rejoin the
main route by proceeding west for a short distance on the A82 and
crossing the stile at the marker post. Continue uphill on the old
Military Road to the junction near the gate, from which the West
Highland Way continues northwards. The path climbs gradually to
a vantage-point from which excellent views are obtained over Strath
Fillan to the north, and of Glen Dochart with the sentinels Ben
More, Stobinian, and Cruach Ardrain to the south-east. Although
the walker has unrestricted views at present, these will no doubt be
reduced as the trees mature.

   The path holds its height and turns northwards to descend over
the Herive Burn; it climbs again for a few yards before following an
old track down to the Oban railway line. The path hugs the fence,
then drops under the railway bridge. After a further few hundred
yards you reach the road at a stile; a little further on cross the main
road and drop down to the Kirkton Bridge. Cross the River Fillan
and walk towards Kirkton Farm. The land in this area is used by the
West of Scotland College of Agriculture for various long-term
cattle- and sheep-breeding schemes, and walkers are asked to make
every effort to minimize livestock disturbance, particularly during
calving and lambing seasons.

St Fillan's Chapel
Near Kirkton Farm, half hidden in a group of trees, are the ruins of
St Fillan's Chapel or Priory. Although badly neglected and almost
unknown to most Scots people, it is of considerable historical
interest. The route skirts the fence adjoining it.

   After St Columba and his companions settled in Iona in 563 AD,
the Christian religion began to spread over Scotland. About the end
of the seventh century, St Fillan, who had made his way south from
Iona, Christianised this area, and according to tradition his original
monastic settlement was situated on the farm of Auchtertyre, near
the Holy Pool. The existing ruin only dates back to the fourteenth
century and was built at the time of Robert the Bruce; he is reputed
to have founded an Augustinian Priory here as a thanksgiving for
his escape from the MacDougalls at the Battle of Dail Righ, or
King's Field, which is about $1\frac{1}{2}$ miles (2.41 kms) away and which the

West Highland Way will pass later.

Many of the stones of the Priory were used to build the
farmhouse and the buildings attached to it. Parts of the north and
south walls of the Priory are still standing and the foundations of
other walls, overgrown with grass, may still be traced. A slab in the
centre of the chapel is believed to cover the grave of the saint.
Immediately to the north of the ruin there is a small graveyard
enclosed by four square walls. The position of the graveyard in
relation to the chapel suggests an older origin for this site than
Roman Catholic times, when graveyards were invariably placed to
the south and west of the church. Several of the graves are covered
with flat stones which were probably taken from the floor of the
chapel; there are also some interesting eighteenth-century
gravestones.

The Relics of St Fillan

A peculiar and romantic interest is attached to relics of the saint,
especially to his crozier and bell, both of which have been preserved
for us in a most extraordinary manner. Not long after his death, the
relics of St Fillan were given in trust to laymen living in
Glendochart, and each man was also given a free grant of land from
the Crown because of his obligations as a custodian. The relics came
to be regarded with awe and reverence and even superstition.

The Crozier, or staff, of St Fillan is known as the Quigrich, which
means a stranger or foreigner. It received this name because it was
carried to distant places for the recovery of stolen property. During
the years of agricultural depression which followed the Battle of
Waterloo, the then custodian of the Quigrich, Archibald Dewar,
left Scotland and emigrated to Canada taking the precious relic with
him. The ancient crozier was kept in a remote prairie clearing and it
is said that Canadian Highlanders who had known of its healing
virtues in the old homeland used to come from far and wide to
procure water in which it had been dipped, for the curing of sick
cattle. After much negotiation, the Quigrich was eventually
returned to Scotland.

St Fillan's bell, called the Bernane, had also been placed in the
custody of a dewar, or keeper: of the early history of this relic

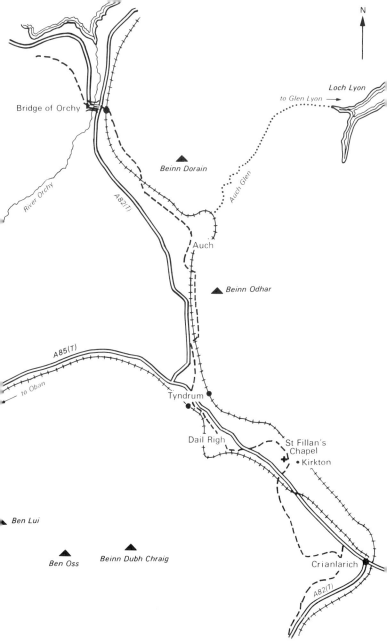

nothing much is known except that it was of sufficient importance to have been borne in the pageant at the coronation of King James IV in 1488. After the Reformation the office of this dewar seems to have disappeared, and for centuries the bell lay exposed to the weather on a tombstone in the churchyard near the ruins of the Priory. It was used in the rites for curing insane people who had been dipped in the Holy Pool of St Fillan. An English tourist, who was staying nearby in August 1798, stole the bell and carried it to Hertfordshire. Its location remained unknown until 1869 when the Bishop of Brechin, who was on a visit to the Earl of Crawford, met a gentleman from England who told him that the bell was owned by a relative of his in Hertfordshire. The Bishop quickly sought out the owner and soon secured the bell for the Society of Antiquaries of Scotland.

Both relics of St Fillan can be seen in the National Museum of Antiquities in Edinburgh.

The Holy Pool and a cure for insanity
After leaving the ruined Priory, the West Highland Way follows a path north-west towards Auchtertyre Farm. Continue on this until it meets the farm road about ½ mile (0.8 kms) later, and take this farm track back towards the River Fillan, crossing the realigned A82 to follow the north bank of the River Fillan. The Holy Pool is in the vicinity of the manse. In this pool the sick were dipped to cure them of their troubles.

Lunatics were brought to the pool from far and near, bound hand and foot and thrown in. At the bottom of the pool there were a number of large pebbles and if the drowning wretch could bring up one of these when he came to the surface, he was regarded as miraculously restored to sanity and the stone was added to a cairn on the bank as a memorial.

Witches too were brought to this Holy Pool and tested in an equally disagreeable way. Their thumbs and great toes were tied together and they were thrown into the water. If they succeeded in scrambling ashore, they were proved witches and were accordingly burned at the stake; if they sank and remained down, then they were innocent and were probably found to be drowned when they were dragged out. Neither way could they win.

The farm road ends a few hundred yards further on, as it joins the old part of the A82 at the north end of the White Bridge over the River Fillan. Cross this road and continue along the riverbank until the junction with the Crom Allt stream. A short distance up this burn, a track crosses it on a sleeper bridge – at the top of the hill beyond, the route turns to the right and leads past a small lochan. The West Highland Way continues northwards to a pine-wood below Tyndrum.

Dail Righ (The Field of the King)

The area around the lochan is called Dail Righ and is the site of Robert the Bruce's second defeat after his coronation, at the hands of MacDougall of Lorn in 1306.

Bruce had been crowned King of Scotland in Scone in March 1306, but in June of that year he had been totally defeated near Methven in Perthshire. With a few brave followers, he had retreated into the Highlands. When he attempted to penetrate into Argyllshire, he found the MacDougalls in arms against him under their chief, John of Lorn. Robert the Bruce was defeated by this chief through sheer force of numbers at Dail Righ.

Tradition has it that Bruce rode away last, covering the retreat, when he was set upon by three MacDougalls. His superior swordsmanship and the narrowness of the ground helped Bruce and he cut the three of them down, but one of the MacDougalls retained in his dying grasp the King's cloak, which was fastened with a brooch. In order to escape, Robert the Bruce unfastened the brooch and released the cloak. This famous Brooch of Lorn is still preserved by the family, MacDougall of Lorn, as a memorial.

Tyndrum

Tyndrum (Tigh an Droma – House of the Ridge) is a small community but in the summer months it becomes an extremely popular tourist village. It is a busy road junction, one road (the A82) continuing north to Fort William and the other (A85) north-west to Oban; it also boasts two railway stations at different levels – 'The Upper' serving the line from Glasgow to Fort William and

Mallaig. 'The Lower' the line from Glasgow to Oban.

Looking back in the direction from which you have been walking, Strath Fillan opens before you with a fine prospect of the Crianlarich Hills. Ben Lui lying south-west from the village has dominated the view on the approach to Tyndrum; it is claimed to be among the most beautiful mountains in the Southern Highlands, particularly with its winter garb of snow. The mountain is renowned for its snow climbs, especially in the Central Gully.

Tyndrum makes an excellent walking and touring centre: there are two hotels; two excellent restaurants, one of which is open all year round; and other accommodation is available in the village. It is advisable to replenish your food from the well-stocked general store because this is the last shop before you reach Kinlochleven. There is also a tourist information service available in the village during the summer months.

The once-famous lead mines were accidentally discovered in 1741 by Sir Robert Clifton, and were worked continuously until 1862. Since then they have fallen into an abandoned state; transport costs proved the biggest difficulty.

In order to resume the route from Tyndrum, go round to the back of the village shop and take the old Glencoe road northwards. Looking back, the spoil-heaps of the old lead-mine workings are clearly visible on the hill slopes on the far side of the Oban road.

Auch

From Tyndrum to Bridge of Orchy, the West Highland Way follows the natural line of the old Glencoe road as it hugs first the base of Beinn Odhar and then Beinn Dorain, with the West Highland Railway running parallel for most of the distance. About 1 mile (1.61 kms) from Tyndrum at a railway bridge crossing the Crom Allt, there is a nice spot for one or two tents. Continue past this bridge on the east side of the railway track until you reach the summit which marks the regional boundary between Central and Strathclyde. The route follows the east side of the railway for another $\frac{1}{2}$ mile (0.81 kms) approximately, where a sheep-creep allows you to pass below the railway in order to rejoin the old road. The signposting is poor and you may experience a little difficulty locating this sheep-creep.

The view to the north of this stretch is dominated by the beautiful cone-shaped Beinn Dorain. The greatest of all the Gaelic poets, Duncan Ban MacIntyre, wrote a long poem about Beinn Dorain and its denizens, the red deer:

> And sweeter to my ear
> Is the concert of the deer
> In their roaring,
> Than when Erin from her lyre
> Warmest strains of Celtic fire
> May be pouring.
> And no organ sends a roll
> So delightful to my soul
> As the branchy-crested race
> When they quicken their proud pace
> And bellow in the face
> Of Ben Dorain.

The red deer were a passion of Duncan Ban's, the hunter bard of Glenorchy, and if you come this way in winter you may see them, monarchs of the glen, as proud now as they were when portrayed on Victorian drawing-room walls.

Approaching Auch there is a good view of the Horse-Shoe Viaduct which carries the railway line above the entrance to Auch Glen; it is a good example of the difficulties which railway engineers overcame when the West Highland Railway was built at the end of the nineteenth century.

Another interesting architectural feature is the old Military Road bridge at the Allt Chonoghlais when you reach the estate cottages at Auch. It is an eighteenth-century segmented arch random rubble structure. Cross the Allt Chonoghlais and walk along the old road which skirts the base of Beinn Dorain. Follow the track for another $3\frac{1}{2}$ miles (5.63 kms); it is in good condition except for the last mile (1.61 kms) which is rather stony. Arriving at Bridge of Orchy railway station, take the station road to the small village of Bridge of Orchy.

The section from Tyndrum to Bridge of Orchy is one of the most pleasant of the entire route as it is easy walking and offers wide vistas in the north-west to Stob Ghabhar and other giants in the Black Mount range. Shortly before reaching Bridge of Orchy Station the walker can obtain views south-westward down the fascinating Glen Orchy.

Accommodation
In addition to the accommodation in Tyndrum mentioned above, there is a comfortable hotel at Bridge of Orchy, which is open all year; there are also a few cottages at Auch and Bridge of Orchy which cater for bed and breakfast. Restricted camping is allowed at Bridge of Orchy but you must obtain permission from the hotel.

Suggestions for additional walks in this section
Walk No 1 Auch to Bridge of Orchy, via Loch Lyon – 20 miles (32.19 kms)
Leave the West Highland Way at Auch and walk up Auch Gleann; the track fords the Allt Chonoghlais at several points and peters out before reaching the ruined cottage of Ais-an-t-Sithein after 3 miles (4.83 kms). Duncan Ban MacIntyre – the famous Gaelic bard – lived here for several years when he was herdsman to the Earl of Breadalbane.

From the ruin of Ais-an t-Sithein a track leads westwards to Loch Lyon after another 3 miles (4.83 kms). Follow the track along Loch Lyon for 2 miles (3.22 kms) and when it reaches the Allt Meran, head north-eastwards up Gleann Meran, crossing the wastershed and proceeding north down the Allt Learg Mheuran to Gorton Halt on the railway. Follow the track westwards to the Gorton bothy, and go down to Achallader Farm and out on to the main road beyond Achallader: 3 miles (4.83 kms) of hard road-walking (south) lies ahead before you return to the West Highland Way at Bridge of Orchy.

Pleast note this walk should not be attempted unless you are experienced in map and compass work because there are parts *en route* where there is no track.

Beinn Dorain

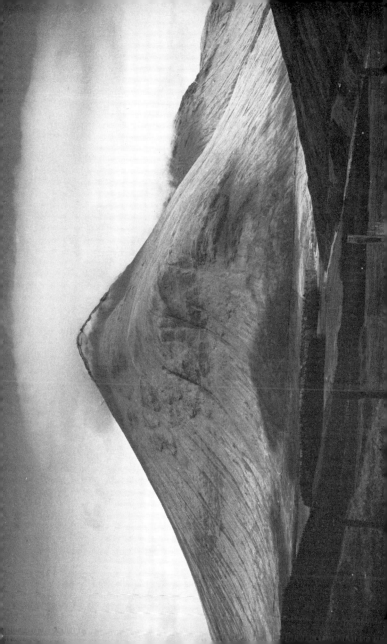

Walk No 2 Auch to Glen Lyon – Distance variable according to inclination.

The first part of this walk is the same as for Walk 1 but after reaching the northern end of Loch Lyon, turn east into Glen Lyon. There is a right of way from Auch to Glen Lyon as this was once the funeral route for the MacGregors of Glen Lyon to their clan burial-ground at Glenorchy Church near Dalmally. This part is trackless as the old right of way has been flooded, and you must make a diversion up Gleann Meran to get round an arm of the loch. The motor road in Glen Lyon now starts at Loch Lyon dam.

Glen Lyon is reputed to be the most beautiful glen in the Southern Highlands and ranks with Glen Affric even as the finest glen in the whole of Scotland. It is almost 30 miles long (48.28 kms) and too big to explore in its entirety as an excursion from the West Highland Way.

If you have the time to walk its length, however, the village of Fortingall near the foot of the glen has many features of interest, including the oldest tree in Europe – a yew tree reputed to be over 3,000 years old, growing in the churchyard. Fortingall is also supposed to be the birthplace of Pontius Pilate. The Romans were certainly stationed in this vicinity.

Suggestions for climbs in this section
Ben Lui – 3,708 ft (1130 m)
The best approach to Ben Lui is along the River Cononish from Dail Righ or Tyndrum. The path ends shortly after Cononish Farm at the Allt an Rund; a small stream comes down from Coire Gaothaich – the beautiful north-east corrie of Ben Lui – and you climb up beside this stream. After entering the corrie there is a choice: go left or right to reach either ridge of the corrie. They are easily climbed in summer. Ascending by either ridge you can climb easily to the summit.

Ben Oss – 3,374 ft (1028 m)
There are several approaches to Ben Oss but one of the most

Ben Lui and Cononish farm

pleasant is from the south. From Inverarnan walk along the main road for about 2 miles (3.22 kms) in Glen Falloch until you reach the Allt Fionn Ghlinne. The stream can be followed right up to Loch Oss, where Ben Oss is easily climbed. This hill is usually climbed in conjunction with Beinn Dubhchraig – 3,204 ft (977 m) – as the col between the two is quite straightforward.

Beinn Odhar – 2,948 ft (898 m)
Although Beinn Odhar is not a noteworthy climb, the view is rewarding. The quickest route is to leave the main road (A82) at a bridge over the railway 1 mile (1.61 kms) north of Tyndrum on the West Highland Way, and follow a faint track almost all the way to the summit; this ascent takes little more than an hour. The view from the summit takes in most of the high tops of Perthshire and Argyllshire.

Beinn Dorain – 3,524 ft (1,074 m)
The usual approach to Beinn Dorain is from Bridge of Orchy. Cross the railway line at the station and go up the south side of the Allt Coire an Dothaidh. After 1 mile (1.61 kms) of steep ascent, turn south and climb up the broad north ridge. Eventually a large cairn is reached, beyond which there is a short drop and then a final ascent leads to the summit, where there is a smaller cairn.

An alternative route of ascent is from Auch; although it is shorter, the climbing is steeper. If you wish to tackle Beinn Dorain from Auch, it is better to walk up Auch Glen for about 1½ miles (2.41 kms) and proceed up the Coire Chruitein, which gives a little scrambling at its head.

Beinn an Dothaidh (pronounced Ben Doe) – 3,267 ft (996 m)
The ascent of Beinn an Dothaidh can be easily made from Bridge of Orchy and is the same route as described for Beinn Dorain, up the Allt Coire an Dothaidh; in fact the two mountains can be climbed together. After reaching the col at the head of Coire an Dothaidh, turn northwards, and a fairly easy climb brings you to the summit plateau.

Leaving Bridge of Orchy Hotel, turn left and walk across the bridge which gives this community its name. The bridge is a scheduled Ancient Monument and is described as being a hump-backed, segmental arch random rubble bridge dating back to 1742.

There is an interesting anecdote about the bridge from Neil Munro's book, *John Splendid*. It concerns the signal which John Splendid saw lying on the glenside keystone, when he was fleeing after the Battle of Inverlochy. 'Three sprigs of gale, a leaf of ivy from the bridge arch where it grew in dark green sprays of glossy sheen and a bare twig of oak standing up at a slant, were held down on the parapet by a peeled willow withy, one end of which pointed in the direction of the glen – the whole held together by two stones.' The message was clear enough to him. The three sprigs of gale meant three men of the Campbell clan; the oak meant a Stewart who was always reminding the Campbells that his race was royal; the ivy leaf meant a Gordon; the peeled branch of willow meant men in a hurry and the twig of oak pointed to the position of the sun. Five fugitives of these names hurrying south over the Bridge of Orchy at 3 o'clock in the afternoon!

A Highlander's name, his clan, his tribal allegiance, were declared by the sprig of plant he wore in his bonnet or tied to the staff of his standard, rather than by the difference in coloured tartan, which came later in the nineteenth century. (See Appendices II and III.)

After crossing the River Orchy go through a large gate in the fence – the gate is not padlocked. There is forestry planting on either side of the track. The observant walker will see evidence on the track that there is a good solid stone foundation and this is part of Major Caulfield's Military Road. It was scheduled as an Ancient Monument as far as Inveroran.

Half a mile on (0.81 kms) a second fence is reached, where a stile is provided. The track continues for a few hundred yards through recently planted forest until a second stile is reached. On crossing this stile the track doubles back on itself but soon resumes its original direction as it curves round the base of Beinn Invereigh.

When the path reaches the top of the rise, splendid views reward the walker. The massif of Stob Ghabhar (the Hill of the Goats) is in

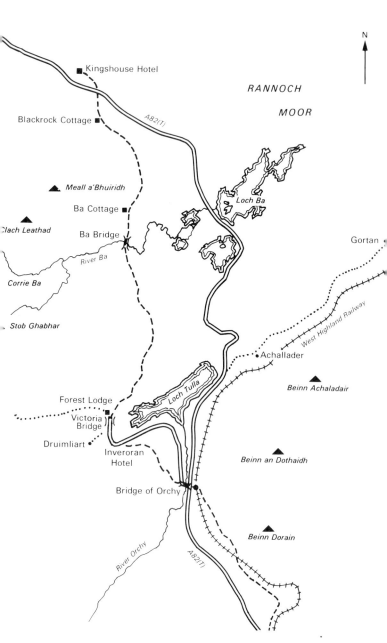

front with Stob Coir an Albannaich (the Highlandman's Peak) and other giants of Glen Etive to the west; in the foreground below is Loch Tulla and the top of the wood of Doire Darach. The Doire Darach is a native pinewood and there are magnificent examples of the old Scots pine contained in it. Beinn Achaladair and Beinn an Dothaidh are seen to the east, and southwards is Beinn Dorain. The track gently zigzags down to the comfortable Inveroran Hotel, which nestles in a picturesque setting among pine trees and close to beautiful Loch Tulla.

Inveroran Hotel
The hotel is a link with the old coaching days when a service between Fort William and Glasgow via Glencoe was started in 1843, the Loch Lomond part of the journey being made by steamer. The coaching service ran from the middle of June to the middle of October. There was an earlier inn here but it was only a thatched house without a sign. William and Dorothy Wordsworth stayed here during their tour of Scotland in 1803. In her journal, Dorothy describes vividly the scene inside:

> Seven or eight drovers with as many dogs were sitting in a complete circle round a large peat fire in the middle of the floor, each with a mess of porridge in a wooden vessel on his knees. A pot suspended from one of the black beams was boiling on the fire. Two or three women were pursuing their household duties on the outside of the circle, while children played on the floor. There was nothing uncomfortable in this confusion; happy and busy faces – all looked pleasant.

At Inveroran, a cattle-drove stance existed for many years, as it was on one of the main drove-routes from Skye and Lochaber to the trysts at Crieff and Falkirk. In 1844 Lord Breadalbane proposed to close the stance-ground, offering in its place another site near Tyndrum. Faced with a change which threatened to make the crossing of the Moor of Rannoch impossible for a drove, the drovers were forced into a lawsuit. The outcome of this action was the provision of a stance at Bridge of Orchy on Achallader Farm,

the tenant of which is still bound by his lease to keep this stance-ground open.

On leaving Inveroran, the route follows the motor road for about 1 mile (1.61 kms) to Victoria Bridge.

Druimliart and Duncan Ban MacIntyre

For anyone interested, it is worth making a short diversion from the road on a cart track to the left just before reaching Victoria Bridge. Walk along this track for about 1 mile (1.61 kms) as it climbs along the side of a little hill into Glen Fuar and on to Druimliart, or Druimlaighart, which is a place-name rather than a place, as there is no habitation there now. Only a few stones remain of an old ruin of special appeal to all Highlanders and those interested in Gaeldom. This was the humble birthplace and home of Duncan Ban MacIntyre – his Gaelic nickname was Donachadh Ban nan Oran (Fair-haired Duncan of the Songs). He could neither read nor write, as schooling was practically non-existent in this lonely region in his day. Most of his songs and descriptive poetry were composed and committed to memory on the rough mountain slopes of Beinn Dorain and the Buachaille Etive Mor, when he was game-keeper to the Earl of Breadalbane. It was left to other Gaelic scholars to write them down from oral tradition.

He was the greatest of all the Gaelic poets and was born here on 20 March 1724. Perhaps in the years to come a commemorative cairn could be erected to his memory on this site.

Victoria Bridge and Forest Lodge

The Victoria Bridge over the Linne nam Beathach, is described as a nineteenth-century double segmental arch bridge with dressed cut-waters. This was the first area in which Queen Victoria stayed in her search for a summer residence in the Highlands. Crossing the bridge, the motor road ends at Forest Lodge. There is a signpost erected by the Scottish Rights of Way Society, which points out the

Bridge of Orchy with Coire an Dothaidh in background

River Orchy (overleaf)

Inveroran Hotel (overleaf)

public footpath westwards to Loch Etive by Glen Kinglass.

The West Highland Way route, however, continues past Forest Lodge where a signboard signifies the route as follows: Drove road to Glencoe. No vehicles.

The track over the next 2 miles (3.22 kms) is very rough but gradually improves when the forestry plantation on the east side terminates. Soon you reach the reed-fringed Lochan Mhic Pheadair Ruaidh. Good views of Clach Leathad (the Stone Hill) to the west and shapely Ben Toaig a little behind to the south-west are obtained from this point.

The going is pleasant now with a feeling of remoteness making it hard to believe that this stretch was once the main road to Glencoe. Within 1 mile (1.61 kms) the picturesque Ba Bridge comes into view.

Corrie Ba

It is worth pausing at this well positioned bridge to admire the River Ba and gaze up to Corrie Ba, which is reputed to be the largest corrie in Scotland.

In 1621 during the reign of James VI (James I of Great Britain), a deer-hunting party observed a pure white hind in the corrie and the Earl of Mar, who was in charge of the party, thought the fact worth reporting to his sovereign, one of whose passions was hunting. King James took it into his head to have the white hind taken alive and sent to England, to Windsor Park. The man designated for this mission was a Mr John Scandaver – an English forester reputed to be expert in the catching of wild deer. The Earl of Mar, who knew the area well, was disturbed by the King's order and by Scandaver's evident confidence of carrying it out in the middle of a hard Scottish winter.

The adventures of Mr Scandaver and his two assistants are well narrated in Sir James Fergusson's essay, 'The White Hind'. They were lucky to escape with their lives after being caught in a severe storm, and the white hind was left to enjoy her freedom.

Perhaps there was a deeper reason why James VI wished to have

Old Glencoe Road, near Victoria Bridge

the white hind captured and brought to him at Windsor. The King was extremely interested in witchcraft and he even had written a book on the subject, *Daemonologie*, published in 1597. The white hind was a creature very closely associated with the Old Religion.

Moor of Rannoch

Another mile (1.61 kms) brings you near the ruin of Ba Cottage and if you look eastwards, the mysterious beauty of the Moor of Rannoch lies before you. Loch Buidhe, Lochan-na-Stainge, Lochan-na-h-Achlaise, Loch Ba, the bends of the River Ba and the numerous other lochans glitter like sapphires if there is a blue sky above.

I think R.L. Stevenson does the moor an injustice when he says, 'A wearier desert man never saw'. He was, however, describing it in order to obtain a dramatic effect in the flight of Alan Breck and David Balfour in his classic *Kidnapped*. The moor can be very dangerous to the unwary but the West Highland Way only skirts the fringe and the track is good to Kingshouse Inn. At the end of this chapter a walk across the moor is described for those more venturesome.

Rannoch Moor is one of the largest moors in Britain covering an area of almost 60 square miles (155.4 sq kms). It is roughly triangular in shape and its boundaries include the old Glencoe road, which is part of the West Highland Way, and the Black Mount in the west; the line of the Black Corries in the north and the Achaladair group and the high ground that continues to Loch Rannoch in the south-east.

During the phases of the Ice Age the moor was ice-covered and fed by glaciers which flowed down from the ice-caps of the surrounding heights. From the Moor the ice spilled over along what are now the main drainage lines. In the north-west and south-west corners the river-flow is to the Atlantic by way of the Etive and the Orchy. The main drainage pattern, however, runs eastwards, starting with innumerable burns which rise in the heart of the Black Mount and unite to form the River Ba. This river crosses 2 miles

Black Mount from Rannoch Moor

(3.22 kms) of moorland from Corrie Ba before cutting below our route at Ba Bridge and through a miniature gorge of red granite slabs. After this the Ba flows in picturesque meanders to the island-studded network of Lochan na Stainge and Loch Ba; then the Abhainn Ba, Loch Laidon, the River Gaur, Loch Rannoch, the Tummel and the Tay finally bring the water to the North Sea.

After the Ice Age, the Moor was extensively wooded, and surviving fragments of the old pine forest may be seen in the Black Wood of Crannach and fringing Loch Tulla. Roots and stumps of former giant firs can still be seen in the peat hags, evidence that this unclad waste was once covered by a mighty race of trees – the ancient Caledonian Forest. Although the wood may have been buried in the soaking moss for a thousand years, it burns like a torch; not only has the bed of peat preserved it from decay, but the old pine roots retain their resin and oils. The Forestry Commission have now replanted areas of the Moor.

In summer the purple heather, the green mosses, yellows and golds of the grasses and the rich browns of the peat hags all combine beautifully. Winter has its own attraction in colour if a clear, frosty day is chosen to cross part of the Moor. It can provide inspiration to the artist in its solitude and expanse, but there are many incidents related concerning the Moor and its dangers in winter.

About 2 miles (3.22 kms) from the ruin of Ba Cottage a small cairn may be seen on the left; the inscription reads: Peter Fleming, Author, Soldier & Traveller, 18 August, 1971.

For some time the Flemings had rented estates in Scotland for shooting holidays and eventually Peter Fleming's grandfather bought the Black Mount estate. Although he enjoyed stalking and shooting, Peter Fleming's chief delight was long, solitary expeditions to the highest and remotest parts of the deer forest; and on 18 August 1971, while shooting with a party, he suffered a sudden heart attack and died in an area which he had loved from a boy into manhood.

The route has now risen to a height of 1,450 ft (442 m) and sweeps down to Kingshouse Inn. Ahead rises the majestic rock face of

South of Ba Bridge, Beinn Achaladair in right background

Buachaille Etive Mor (the big hersdman of Etive), which like a sentinel guards the entrances to Glencoe and Glen Etive. The Way passes Blackrock Cottage which belongs to the Ladies Scottish Climbing Club, and behind to the north the White Corries ski station can be seen. Cross the main road (A82) and continue the short distance to Kingshouse by the old Glencoe road.

Kingshouse Inn

This was formerly a coaching inn and it is believed to date back to about 1750. Travellers of the eighteenth and early nineteenth centuries record that the innkeeper sat rent free and had an annual government grant. It certainly served a need in this lonely region, offering shelter and refreshment to drovers, soldiers and travellers of every sort before they began the long journey southward, skirting the dangerous edge of the Moor of Rannoch.

Can we imagine what deeds have been done at Kingshouse in years gone by? Red-coated soldiers hunting clansmen; wild drovers with their cattle; adventurers like Alan Breck and John Splendid spending a night at Kingshouse, dirk and pistol at the ready? Here we are in the very centre of the romance and mystery of the Moor of Rannoch.

In more recent times Kingshouse has become very popular with the outdoor fraternity. The hotel is now extended and the interior modernised.

Accommodation

The small hotel at Inveroran is only open from Easter until the middle of October, but Kingshouse Hotel is open all year. Advance booking is strongly recommended for both, even in the winter months, as Kingshouse is very busy with skiers. There are good camping sites near Inveroran Hotel and Victoria Bridge but permission must be sought first from Forest Lodge.

Suggestions for additional walks in this section
Walk No 1 Bridge of Orchy to Loch Rannoch – 23 miles (37.02 kms)

Ba Bridge

This was an important drove-route. After leaving Bridge of Orchy, walk along the main motor road (A82) for the first mile (1.61 kms) and then take the old road on the right-hand side for another mile (1.61 kms). Along this part of the old road you will see a cairn, with an inscription: 'Battle of Legando – 1468 – to commemorate the bond of allegiance between the Fletchers of Achallader and the Stewarts of Appin. They died here each for the other.' The old road joins the A82 which you walk along until you reach Loch Tulla.

Take the Achallader Farm road on the right and walk up to the farm and ruined castle. It was from the old castle of Achallader that, on that awful wintry day in February 1692, Campbell of Glen Lyon treacherously led the Government troops over to Glencoe to do their bloody work there on the unfortunate MacDonalds.

A mile (1.61 kms) beyond this, the track crosses the water of Tulla at Barravourich (now a ruin) and follows the north side of the water for another 3¼ miles (5.23 kms), passing the old pine woods of Crannach which lie on the other side, until it reaches the cottage at Gorton.

About 2 miles (3.22 kms) beyond Gorton the route goes under the railway to a mossy place (Madagan Moineach) where the droves generally rested for the night. It then runs north-east over the Moor, crossing some half-dozen small streams flowing north, the last of which is the Allt Beithe Beag, and passes about the 1,400 ft-level (428 m) to the north-west of the hill Meall Leachdann nan Each (the stone slope for the horses), about 4 miles (6.44 kms) east of Madagan Moineach. You are now at the head of Gleann Chomraidh. Bearing rather more north, you will reach the cottage of Grunnd nan Darachan from which a good road leads down the west side of the glen to Invercomrie and Bridge of Gaur, at the west end of Loch Rannoch and 6 miles (9.66 kms) east of Rannoch railway station, where there is a small hotel. Accommodation is

Placid waters of Loch Tulla

Kingshouse Hotel with Buachaille Etive Mor in the background (overleaf)

Blackrock Cottage with Buachaille Etive Mor in background (overleaf)

very limited in this area and you should be prepared to camp out.

Walk No 2 Rannoch Station to Kingshouse Hotel – 12 miles (19.31 kms)
To cross the Moor of Rannoch take the train from Bridge of Orchy to Rannoch, the next station north on the West Highland Railway line.

Leaving Rannoch Station, the moorland walk begins round the head of Loch Laidon; for the first 1½ miles (2.41 kms) or so the route is near the north shore of the loch but afterwards keeps well above it. Then go west-by-south to the ruined cottage of Tigh na Cruaiche, a green oasis on the moor, about 4 miles (6.44 kms) from the railway station. Then strike due west away from the Loch, first rising slightly then descending again to Black Corries Lodge at the foot of Meall nan Ruddhag, from which there is a road 3 miles (4.83 kms) to Kingshouse Hotel.

This is rather a difficult route to follow owing to the very rough and boggy country. It is unrelieved by any good landmarks for guidance; it is advisable to attempt it only in dry and clear weather. Good visibility is important for this route, as it is risky crossing the Moor in misty weather.

As an alternative to walking this whole section of the West Highland Way, walks 1 and 2 can be combined so that you leave the route at Bridge of Orchy and rejoin it again at Kingshouse Hotel; this allows the more adventurous walker to cross Rannoch Moor. The total distance for this combination is 41 miles (66 kms) as it includes almost 6 miles (9.66 kms) of road walking from Bridge of Gaur to Rannoch Station.

Before we leave this section on the Moor of Rannoch, there are many incidents which can be related concerning the Moor and its dangers in winter but one which is remarkable concerns a shepherd and his dogs:

One winter's morning, some years ago, a shepherd left home with his two collies for the hilly region south of Loch Rannoch. The ground was snow-covered and the weather stormy. It was not a day

Old Glencoe Road

for the high tops but the man was anxious about the safety of some of his sheep in the outlying corries. When he was 5 miles away from his house, a blizzard blew up, and even with his intimate knowledge of the area the shepherd at last lost his way.

What happened next showed the sublime devotion of the collies for their master, and also the wisdom of dogs. One of the collies made his way home through the deep snow. When the dog reached the shepherd's house, he showed by his agitation and actions that he urgently wished people to follow him. A search-party started off and the collie guided them unerringly through the snow to the spot where his unconscious master was lying. The search party found the second dog, dead, lying on his master's chest to give him all the warmth and shelter possible.

It was obvious the two collies must have conferred before deciding on their course of action in the emergency which confronted them. The shepherd recovered and lived – thanks to his dogs.

Suggestions for additional climbs in this section
In severe winter conditions, the following climbs should only be undertaken by a properly equipped party of experienced hill-climbers.

Stob Ghabhar – 3,556 ft (1,086 m), lies to the north-west of Loch Tulla and is most easily approached from Forest Lodge. The public track to Glen Kinglass and Loch Etive should be followed for about 1 mile (1.61 kms) to Clashgour (the Glasgow University Mountaineering Club Hut), which was formerly a schoolhouse. At the hut a well-made subsidiary track turns off up the Allt Toaig ascending gradually and contouring the slopes of Beinn Toaig and Stob a' Choire Odhair, then cutting back to zigzag up the shoulder of the latter. This path should be left near the 1,000 ft (305 m) contour. Crossing the burn, bear left to ascend the south-east ridge

Loch Tulla with Stob Ghabhar in background
Clach Leathad and Meall a'Bhuiridh from Rannoch Moor (overleaf)
Kingshouse Hotel with Sron na Creise in background (overleaf)

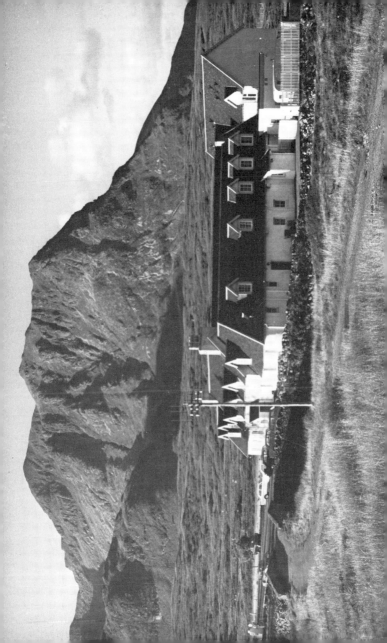

of Stob Ghabhar to reach the cairn.

If you wish to continue along the ridge to Clach Leathad, 3,602 ft (1,098 m), keep to the edge of the precipices and walk downhill to Sron nan Giubhas and continue along the ridge of Aonach Mor. This rises gently in a north-westerly direction. After about 1 mile (1.61 kms) turn right and descend the spur for about 500 ft (152 m) to the Bealach Fuarchathaidh, the lowest point on the ridge. A steep climb of some 1,200 ft (366 m) brings you to the summit cairn of Clach Leathad.

You can continue along this magnificent ridge by walking due north for nearly 2 miles (3.22 kms) of level ground to attain Stob a' Ghlais Choire. A little scrambling brings you to Sron na Creise, 2,952 ft (900 m), the terminal point on the ridge. Descend to the left of its long shoulder to negotiate the buttress in safety, and contour round its lower slopes to Kingshouse Hotel.

From Clach Leathad the ridge walk can be shortened by crossing to Meall a'Bhuiridh, 3,636 ft (1,108 m), whose lower slopes may be descended by the White Corries Chairlift.

Meall a'Bhuiridh is one of the main skiing centres in Scotland, as its north-facing slopes hold the snow well. The Scottish Ski Club erected a tow in 1955 on the top 900 ft (274 m) of the mountain; Scotland's first commercial ski company, White Corries Ltd, put in a chairlift in 1960 and a second tow in 1963. The chairlift now operates in summer as well as in winter, weather permitting.

Clach Leathad and Meall a'Bhuiridh

Although the West Highland Way only touches the entrances to both glens Coe and Etive and actually by-passes both, they are so famed for their wild beauty and historical associations that I feel they deserve a chapter to themselves in this guide. They also contain some of the best climbing areas in the British Isles. The walker taking the main route may not have the time to explore the fastnesses of either glen, and can then skip this chapter altogether.

Glencoe
In 1935 and 1937 the finest part of Glencoe was acquired by the National Trust for Scotland and it is held in perpetuity for the nation. The boundaries of this area are – the north ridge of Glencoe from above Clachaig Inn to Altnafeadh, the River Coupal to its junction with the River Etive and along the latter to Dalness, thence north-west by the ridge of Bidean nam Bian to Clachaig. The total area is about twenty square miles, and free and unrestricted access to all the mountains, corries and glens is permitted at all times.

There is a Visitor Centre at the west end of the glen, built by the Countryside Commission for Scotland and run by the National Trust; within the building there are light refreshments, toilets and information services. A viewing platform on part of the roof provides good views of the surrounding mountains.

Early history and traditions of Glencoe and Glen Etive
Little has survived of the early history of Glencoe and Glen Etive, either by written record or tradition. Some of the place-names recall ancient Celtic legends, the most famous being that of the beautiful Irish maiden, Deirdre. She fled to Glen Etive from Ulster with her lover Naisi, in order to escape the unwelcome attentions of King Conor. They were lured back to Erin by the treacherous King, there to meet their fate. On leaving Alban (Scotland), Deirdre sings a lament in which she recalls the scenes of her past happiness and recalls the beauty of the woods at sunrise in Glen Etive, where she had made her earliest home.

In Glencoe, Sgor nam Fiannaidh (the peak of the Feinne) recalls the heroes celebrated in the poems attributed to the Bard Ossian, whose own name has become attached to the cave high up on

Aonach Dubh, where he was supposed to have lived in the fifth century AD. This is very doubtful as access to the cave is quite difficult and requires considerable climbing ability.

Tales of the Feinne were widely known and told in the Highlands; they were folk heroes, giants of stature and of deeds, warrior hunters, generous in spirit, brave and given to great hospitality; they had in fact the very qualities which the Gael most admired and the importance of these poems to the Gael was immense.

It is said that Earragan, King of Lochlann, warred against the Feinne. He sailed up Loch Leven to the mouth of the Coe. His men went ashore at Gleann an Fhuidhaich, a level field on the lower part of the Glen. They erected tents about a mile (1.61 kms) from Invercoe House. The Feinne encamped in a thick wood in the lower part of the Glen, now called Sgor nam Fiannaidh. They dug four large ditches on the hillside for defence and living-quarters until they had collected all their people. It was a well-chosen place, for the top of the hill behind them, Sgor na Ciche (known as the Pap of Glencoe), was full of loose stones for throwing and as the way was steep, a few men could keep a larger number at bay with stones. Traces of the four ditches can still be seen halfway up the hill. (See also Appendix IV.)

Glencoe belonged in early clan days first to the MacDougalls, then from the time of Robert Bruce to the MacDonalds. The power of the Clan Donald began to wane and the Glencoe lands were granted by the Crown to the Stewarts of Appin, who therefore under feudal law were the superiors of the MacDonalds. The Campbells, however, became more powerful and eventually in the sixteenth century the Earls of Argyll (Campbells) became the superiors of the Stewarts. The MacDonalds and Campbells hated each other and the MacDonalds often stole cattle from the Campbells. Cattle-raiding was a recognised way of living in the Highlands in those times.

Highland economy was perhaps rudimentary but by no means barbarous – in the anthropological sense. They grew their own corn and in summer and autumn hunting gave them ample game and the fishing was good. Cattle was salted down for the winter and salmon were kippered. They traded their fish and skins for manufactured goods from Lowland Scotland; their famous black cattle were sent in droves to the south. Money circulated and they were not without certain luxuries. They were also not devoid of education and many could speak English and French as well as their native Gaelic.

There were refinements in their lives and also much merriment; the men had athletic events such as fierce games of shinty or races, and the women would spin or dance to the pipes. Their music consisted not only of the pipes but of the harp or clarsach, which was a much older instrument in these Highland glens. (See Appendix V.)

Events leading to the Massacre of Glencoe

The MacDonalds of Glencoe were both Episcopalian in church matters and loyal supporters of the Stewart cause. When the revolution of 1688 drove the Stewarts from the throne, the clan joined Viscount Dundee in his rising on behalf of King James. After Dundee's death in battle the Royalist forces began to break up, and on their homeward journey westwards the MacDonalds plundered the lands of Glenlyon.

In spite of Viscount Dundee's death, the clans who had supported him continued in their allegiance to King James. William III, who was fully engaged in a war with France, was anxious to remove the threat of a Highland uprising should a French invasion materialise and the Government issued a proclamation offering a pardon to all who had been in arms provided that they took the oath of allegiance before 1 January 1692. By the beginning of December, 1691, however, few submissions had been received. The Secretary of State, Sir John Dalrymple, the Master of Stair, stated in a letter that he was beginning to consider an alternative plan to bring the late-comers to heel.

The delaying action of the clan chiefs in making peace with the Government was due partly to a desire to have the consent of King James to their relinquishing their allegiance to him, and partly to their hopes for a French landing in Scotland. MacIan (Chief of the Glencoe MacDonalds) delayed until the very last day. He finally

At the head of Loch Etive – the Land of Deirdre

presented himself before Colonel Hill, the governor of Fort William on 31 December. Hill explained to MacIan that he could not accept his submission as the oath of allegiance could only be administered by a civil magistrate, and he sped the old chief on his way to Inverary with a letter to the sheriff-depute.

MacIan was an old man, however, and his progress was delayed by a snowstorm. When at last he reached Inveraray on 2 January, he found Campbell of Ardkinglass, the sheriff-depute, absent; and when the latter returned on the 5th, he at first hesitated to administer the oath after the required date. He finally agreed on listening to MacIan's earnest pleading, but warned the old chief that his case would have to be referred to the Privy Council in Edinburgh. Campbell wrote, however, to Colonel Hill informing him of what had taken place and asking the Colonel to take MacIan and his followers under his protection. Safe with this knowledge the old chief returned home.

But the Master of Stair – Secretary of State for Scotland to King William – was determined to make an example of the MacDonalds and forwarded the order from the King 'to extirpate that sept of thieves'; later he sent instructions that 'it be secret and sudden'.

On 1 February a company of Argyll's regiment under the command of Captain Robert Campbell of Glenlyon, the victim of the MacDonalds' raid after the Battle of Killiecrankie, appeared in Glencoe and billeted themselves in the various houses of the MacDonalds. It was supposed to be a military exercise. For two weeks the troops enjoyed the hospitality of the MacDonalds, living with them on the best of terms.

On 12 February, 800 soldiers under the command of a Major Duncanson left Fort William to co-operate with Glenlyon in carrying out the Master of Stair's orders, and also to ensure that the escape route via Kinlochleven and the top part of Glencoe (now known as the Devil's Staircase) was sealed. A message was sent on ahead to Glenlyon ordering him to 'putt all to the sword under seventy'. At about 4 or 5 in the morning one of Glenlyon's officers, Lieutenant Lindsay, came with a party of men to the chief's house. After calling out in a friendly manner and so gaining admittance, they shot the old man in the back as he was getting out of bed. They also stripped his wife and drew the rings off her fingers with their teeth.

Up and down the Glen the treacherous work of butchery went on. Those who escaped fled to the hills under cover of a heavy snowstorm which had broken during the night. In all, out of an adult male population of perhaps 150, about 38 men were killed, but the burning of the houses left the people with no shelter and all their livestock were driven off by the troops, so that at least as many more men and women died from exposure and starvation.

In spite of their greatly superior numbers and the advantage of their sudden treacherous attack, the troops had failed completely to carry out their instructions. Even when allowance is made for the effect of the snowstorm, historians now believe some of the soldiers must have helped in the escape of their hosts. It is significant that local traditions of the massacre nearly all tell of individual soldiers trying to convey last-minute warnings to the people or attempting to spare their lives.

The Master of Stair felt no regret when he read Hill's report of the affair. The Secretary of State must have known of MacIan's belated submission at Inveraray. After demands by the Scottish Parliament, King William was forced to set up an enquiry in 1695. The appointed Commission took evidence from the survivors and from such persons concerned as were available. Their conclusions were that there was nothing in the King's instructions to justify the massacre and that the Master of Stair had exceeded these instructions. The Master was deprived of his office of Secretary of State but he was excused by the King from any blame for the barbarous manner of the execution of his orders. He was also granted a pension.

The whole dastardly action left a bitterness in the memories of the Highlanders and there are even faint echoes of it today. The treachery of an enemy accepting hospitality and then putting its hosts to the sword is against every moral principle a man can have.

The later history of Glencoe
Despite the losses suffered in the massacre and later in the Jacobite Risings of 1715 and 1745, the population of the Glen actually

increased and by the end of the eighteenth century there was a
problem of over-population. The later introduction of sheep into
the Highlands had serious effects on the population and many of the
inhabitants were forced to emigrate from Scotland. Much of the
land which formerly had grown corn then became waste.

An inn was built at Clachaig in 1839 and from 1843 a stage-coach
service from Inverness to Glasgow halted there for refreshment. In
1933 the present road through the Glen was opened, despite a great
deal of protest.

Wild life in Glencoe and Glen Etive
The area of the two glens cannot be considered rich in wild life and
this is accounted for by the lack of shelter – there are no large woods
or plantations. The most impressive exception is without doubt the
red deer, and large herds may often be seen. There are wildcats also
in the neighbourhood. The golden eagle can be seen soaring high
above the tops of the mountains and peregrin falcon can also be
spotted in the wilder regions; other birds of prey such as buzzards
are numerous. Above the 2,500 ft (762 m) contour the ptarmigan is
quite plentiful; also at high altitudes the snow bunting may be
heard.

Accommodation
Kingshouse and Clachaig are the nearest hotels for access to
Glencoe and Glen Etive; there are also houses in the village of
Glencoe which offer facilities for bed and breakfast. The Glencoe
Youth Hostel is open all year and has ample accommodation.

Camping in Glencoe is restricted to two official sites – one is just
off the main road a little west of the Visitor Centre and the other is
at Invercoe near the village of Glencoe. There are also good spots
for camping in Glen Etive between the river and road.

Some suggestions for walks and climbs

Glencoe
As stated earlier in this chapter, Glencoe is one of the finest areas
for climbing in the British Isles and only a brief outline can be given

here of ideas for hill-walkers. There are more detailed books for the
enthusiast and I would advise the reader to consult these – the
Scottish Mountaineering Club guides are recommended.

From the Visitor Centre a bridge gives access across the River
Coe to the Clachaig Inn and to woodland walks provided by the
Forestry Commission on 45 acres of neighbouring ground. The walks
lead to Signal Rock about ½ mile (0.81 kms) west of the Centre.
Signal Rock is closely associated with the story of the Massacre of
Glencoe as it was reputed to have been from this rock that the signal
was given for the commencement of the action. Historians doubt
this.

The Lost Valley
A visit to Coire Gabhail – the corrie of capture, or as it is now
known among the climbing fraternity 'The Lost Valley' – is well
worth making for its own sake as it is a perfect example of a hanging
valley. It cannot be seen from the road and the many thousands of
tourists visiting Glencoe are unaware of the existence of a secret
place which is remarkable for its atmosphere of Himalayan
seclusion. It always reminds me of the novel *Lost Horizon* by James
Hilton, and I suspect this was the origin of the current nickname.

The MacDonalds used to drive their cattle up into Coire Gabhail
for safety and no doubt they also hid many more which had been
stolen from their neighbours in this secluded retreat. It must have
been a perfect hideout with its very narrow entrance, beyond which
opens out a beautiful level valley containing good pasture
surrounded on all sides by very steep mountain slopes.

The walk up to it can be started from the bridge over the River
Coe, opposite Allt-na-Reigh cottage, ½ mile (0.81 kms) west of the
Meeting of the Three Waters. A muddy path leads up on the left
bank of the Allt Coire Gabhail and through a deep gorge; it then
crosses to the right bank and proceeds through a maze of tumbled
boulders. The burn disappears under these rocks and reappears on
the base of the corrie higher up. The floor of the corrie stretches for
½ mile (0.81 kms). The steep slopes of Gearr Aonach and Beinn
Fhada rise on either side of the 'Lost Valley' and at its head is the
ridge of Bidean nam Bian.

Glen Etive

Although Glen Etive is not so famous as Glencoe it rivals it in scenic beauty. A narrow road leaves the main road (A82) about 1 mile (1.61 kms) west of Kingshouse Hotel and follows the River Etive down the glen between Buachaille Etive Mor on the right and Sron na Creise on the left to Dalness – distance 7 miles (11.27 kms). There are good camping sites just off the road along this stretch of river, if you wish to explore the glen and its environs. The road terminates at the head of Loch Etive, which is 13 miles (20.92 kms) from the junction with the main road, (A82).

From Dalness, two hill routes cross to Glencoe. The first is by the Lairig Gartain, between Buachaille Etive Mor and Buachaille Etive Beag and it joins the Glencoe Road near Altnafeadh, the distance being 4½ miles (7.24 kms). There is no path through the Lairig Gartain. The second route of 3½ miles (5.63 kms) follows a rough track which goes through the Lairig Eilde between Buachaille Etive Beag and Beinn Fhada and crosses from the west bank of the Allt Lairig Eilde to the east side about ½ mile (0.81 kms) before reaching the Glencoe Road. By either route there is a steep ascent from Dalness to the summits of the two respective passes but the descents are more gradual, although longer, down to Glencoe.

Buachaille Etive Mor, Stob Dearg – 3,345 ft (1,020 m)

The dominating position of Stob Dearg on the approach to Glencoe means that this one summit is popularly identified as the Bauchaille Etive Mor, whereas the Buachaille really consists of a ridge stretching from Stob Dearg for some 2½ miles (4.02 kms) along the west side of Glen Etive to Stob na Broige above Dalness.

Stob Dearg can be ascended by an easy route from Altnafeadh on the Glencoe road. Cross the River Coupall by a foot-bridge, and make your way up the Coire na Tulaich directly opposite. From here after a rough scramble over scree, the summit ridge is gained at the col, 2,900 ft (883 m), about ½ mile (0.81 kms) west of the summit cairn. The walk to the top is quite easy.

The view is not outstanding although it commands a wide

The Buachaille Etive Mor – Sentinel of Glencoe

panorama across the desolate Moor of Rannoch. The sharp cone of Schiehallion is conspicuous; to the north the view is of the Mamores and the Nevis massif.

The descent from Stob Dearg can be made to Glen Etive by continuing west along the summit ridge for about 400 yds (3.6 m) and then striking left down Coire Choiche Finne. In descending it is necessary to bear continuously to the right in order to avoid difficult slopes. The Glen Etive road is joined about 2 miles (3.22 kms) from the main road, (A82). In bad weather this descent should not be attempted and it is safer to go down by the way you came up.

No other routes should be attempted unless by very experienced rock climbers; the Buachaille has claimed many lives and has gained a bad reputation.

Bidean nam Bian – 3,766 ft (1,148 m)
This is the highest mountain in Argyll; it really consists of several closely set peaks, which together are of outstanding interest and character. The summit of Bidean itself is masked by its three northern spurs, which are well known as the 'Three Sisters'. The tops of Bidean are so steep and closely clustered that it is impossible to obtain a satisfactory overall view of them except from high on some more distant peak – from the Mamores, for instance. The actual summit of Bidean itself is so shut off that you can only glimpse it behind the two great rock buttresses, the Diamond and the Church Door, from the floor of Glencoe near Clachaig Inn.

Bidean nam Bian is usually climbed by way of Coire nam Beith, which is probably one of the most varied and interesting routes to the summit. Cross the bridge over the River Coe at the west end of Loch Achtriochtan and follow up the left bank of the stream past several fine waterfalls. A path then leads through a narrow ravine to cross the burn, ½ mile (0.81 kms) farther on at a point where two branches of the stream unite, at approximately 1,750 ft (533 m). Follow the left-hand tributary to the boulder field of the upper corrie; steep scree slopes have to be surmounted on the left before the col between Bidean and Stob Coire nan Lochan is reached. The

Stob Dearg from Altnafeadh

ridge from this col to the summit is narrow and steep, but is not
dangerous except under severe winter conditions.

Whilst descending, care should be taken lest by mistake you
follow one of the short ridges running out to the left to either of the
twin buttresses near the summit. From the saddle an easier slope
leads over to the summit of Stob Coire nan Lochan – 3,657 ft (1,115
m), the ascent of which can be combined with that of Bidean.

The view from the summit is most extensive; to the north, over
the Aonach Eagach ridge on the opposite side of Glencoe, there are
the Mamore mountains with the Nevis range immediately beyond.
From the west round to the south are Loch Linnhe with the hills of
Ardgour and Morven beyond, Ben Bheithir, Ben Cruachan and the
upper reaches of Loch Etive. To the south-east is the Black Mount
group and the more distant mountains in Perthshire. Immediately
to the east is Buachaille Etive Beag with Buachaille Etive Mor
rising behind.

Aonach Eagach Ridge
The traverse of this ridge is graded officially as easy but this can be
misleading and an attempt should certainly not be undertaken by
any party lacking rock-climbing experience. It is extremely unwise
to attempt it solo and the smallest number in a party should be three
members. A rope is indispensable for a party less experienced, and
to a competent party the use of a rope may give useful practice in
moving fast together. Once the actual ridge is begun, there is no
easy way off.

Although the name Aonach Eagach – notched ridge – properly
belongs to the narrow and precipitous central portion, it is also used
to include the whole ridge bounding Glencoe on the north, from the
Pap of Glencoe (Sgor na Ciche) above Loch Leven to the Devil's
Staircase on the line of the old Military Road from Kingshouse to
Fort William.

The Pap of Glencoe, 2,430 ft (741 m) can be climbed from the old
road below the Youth Hostel: from the summit descend to the col
between Sgor na Ciche and Sgor nam Fiannaidh and then climb to
the latter's summit at 3,168 ft (966 m). The slopes are steep and
towards the summit ridge they run into tedious scree. From the

summit (a short distance to the east of the point at which the ridge is reached) the ridge may be followed eastwards for about $\frac{1}{2}$ mile (0.81 kms) to Stob Coire Leith – 3,080 ft (939 m). Beyond this point the ridge becomes narrow and precipitous, frequently projecting into rocky pinnacles. This part continues as far as the ridge known as 'The Chancellor' and then on to Am Bodach – 3,085 ft (940 m), beyond which the ridge becomes broad and easy. The descent from Am Bodach is fairly easy down to the Glencoe road.

From the entire length of the Aonach Eagach ridge magnificent views may be had of Glencoe and Bidean nam Bian opposite as well as the Nevis massif and the Mamore mountains to the north. The traverse provides a memorable expedition in either direction, although it is made more often from east to west in order to enjoy the particularly fine sequence of views out towards the west.

The Three Sisters of Glencoe with Bidean nam Bian in the background (overleaf)

The Aonach Eagach Ridge, Glencoe (overleaf)

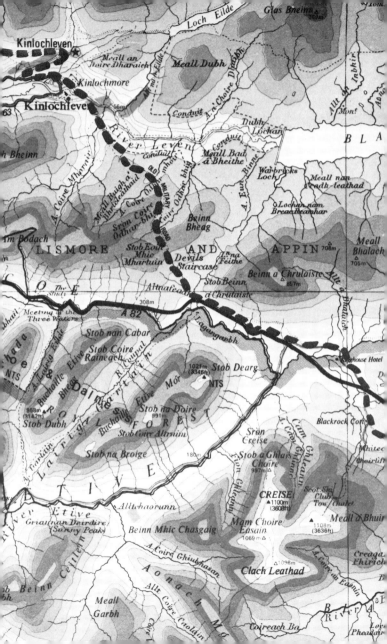

Follow the western access road from Kingshouse Hotel for a little over $\frac{1}{2}$ mile (0.8 kms) and then strike off up the hill to the right on a faint track; the path becomes clearer as it climbs on to the lower slopes of Beinn a' Chrulaiste. The walker is now back on the old Military Road. Continue along this track until it joins the main road and follow the latter to Altnafeadh.

Altnafeadh and the Devil's Staircase
Altnafeadh was formerly a cattle-stance where the drovers rested their cattle for the night on their long way south to the trysts. Our route strikes off from the main road on the right a little beyond the keeper's house and goes uphill to rejoin the old Military Road above the Altnafeadh plantation. The West Highland Way is now following a continuation of the Military Road from Stirling to Fort William, constructed in 1750–52. The old road twists upwards with a series of zigzag bends known as the 'Devil's Staircase'. It is not known how this name originated, but it is an apt one. It is mentioned quite casually by Thomas Telford in his recommendations for the Fifth Report of the Commissioners for Highland Roads and Bridges. Perhaps it was named by the unfortunate Government troops who were committed to construct it, as they sweated and shivered at their task.

Serious gully erosion has caused the track to be very rough. There are annual motor-cycle scrambling events held on the Devil's Staircase and this has undoubtedly contributed to its serious deterioration, especially where wheel-tracks cut across the original, well-graded zigzag bends. It is questionable whether motor-cycling should continue to be permitted in the long-term interests of this important hill pass.

It is worth pausing and looking back occasionally as the track commands very fine views into Glencoe and over to the Black Mount. After about 1 mile (1.61 kms) you will reach the summit cairns at 1,800 ft (549 m). Continuing slowly from the summit cairns, very fine views can be had of the Mamore mountains and the Nevis group to the north, if the visibility is good.

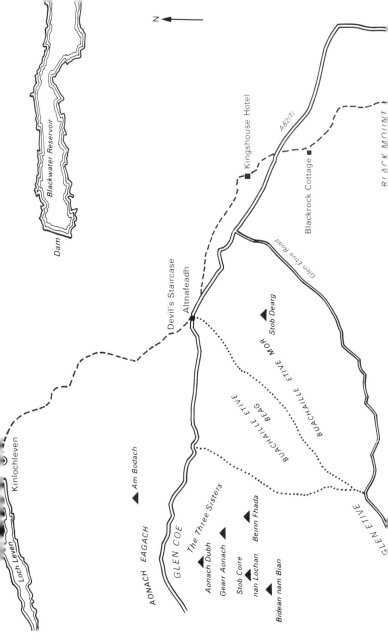

Blackwater Reservoir

As you continue, the broad expanse of the Blackwater Reservoir can be seen away to the right. This is not a natural loch but was constructed between 1904 and 1907 prior to the start of production at the Kinlochleven Aluminium Works. The reservoir is 8 miles (12.88 kms) long and the dam wall itself is over ½ mile (0.81 kms) long, over 60 ft (18.29 m) wide at the base and has an average height of 80 ft (24.38 m). There have been far bigger dams built since then, but one has to remember that this was all pick-and-shovel work. Thousands of labourers were employed on this project and the standard rate of pay was 'A tanner an hour, overtime seven and a half'. Sixpence an hour meant thirty shillings a week and a man was allowed to work overtime until he fell exhausted at his shift.

All year round men used to cross the hills in order to spend some of their pay at Kingshouse Inn. In the winter many died in the snow on the way back to the camp, and stalkers used to find many a nameless corpse when the snow melted in the spring.

As the condition of the track has improved, it is easy walking during the gradual descent. Good views are obtained, on your left, of the north side of the Aonach Eagach ridge. About 2.4 miles (3.9 kms) from the summit, the track joins the access road to Blackwater Reservoir near the power station. The township of Kinlochleven and Loch Leven are in view. The descent to Kinlochleven is approximately 1.8 miles (2.9 kms), and although the surface is good, the path is steep in places.

The Aluminium Works at Kinlochleven

Kinlochleven is reached by passing the Aluminium Works, which are the oldest functioning works in the country. In 1900, Kinlochleven consisted of only about two houses at the head of Loch Leven but the construction of the works changed the area into a town. The thousands of navvies who worked there during the years 1904 to 1907 only spoke of the waterworks – they did not know and cared even less that they were building the largest

The start of the Devil's Staircase, Altnafeadh (overleaf)
On the Devil's Staircase, looking south-east to the Black mount (overleaf)

aluminium factory in Britain at that time.

It certainly has earned a unique place in Highland history: the wild lawlessness, the squalor of their living conditions, the drinking, gambling and fighting – all are reminiscent of the gold rush to the Yukon. An account of this period is very well given in the book, *Children of the Dead End* by Patrick MacGill, an Irish labourer who worked there. Even the nicknames of his work-mates seem to come from the Klondyke rather than a Highland glen – characters like Moleskin Joe, Carroty Dan, Blasting Mick, and Ben the Moocher.

Kinlochleven
All that wild lawlessness is in the past and Kinlochleven is a small quiet town now, with a population of about 1,500. Attempts are being made to make the town a tourist centre. It is certainly a good starting point for exploring the Mamore range of mountains. Unfortunately there is no hotel in the town, but many houses take in visitors for bed, breakfast and evening meal, and from the small tourist information kiosk, open in the summer months, information about accommodation is available.

MacGill's descriptive writing is both philosophical and vivid. Here he describes the country through which you have walked:

> Above and over all, the mystery of the night and the desert places hovered inscrutable and implacable. All around the ancient mountains sat like brooding witches, dreaming on their own story of which they knew neither the beginning nor the end. Naked to the four winds of heaven and all the rains of the world, they had stood there for countless ages in all their sinister strength, undefied and unconquered, until man, with puny hands and little tools of labour, came to break the spirit of their ancient mightiness.

Suggestions for additional walks and climbs in this section
Kinlochleven is a good centre for those hill-walkers who have a few

Summit Cairn on the Devil's Staircase, looking north to the Mamores, Ben Nevis on extreme left

days to spare and it is the best starting-point for all the Mamore
peaks from Am Bodach eastwards.

Walk No 1 Circular from Kinlochleven to Loch Treig – 22 miles
(35.4 kms)
Walk eastwards from Kinlochleven up the north bank of the River
Leven to the Blackwater reservoir. About ½ mile (0.81 kms) along
the reservoir the path runs north-east along the Allt an Inbhir and
then along the Allt an Ruadha Dheirg to Loch Chiarain at the
mouth of a deep and narrow pass, which was an old drove-route.
Walk through the pass and down Gleann Iolainean to
Lochtreighead.

   To circle back to Kinlochleven, turn left when you reach the track
at Loch Treig and walk towards Creaguaineach Lodge; cross the
bridge over the Amhainn Rath and turn left before you reach the
lodge on to a path which follows the river for about 4 miles (6.44
kms) up to the house at Luibeilt. At Luibeilt follow the track south,
passing Lochs Eilde Beag and Eilde Mor on their northern banks,
and continue south-west, descending steeply to Mamore Lodge and
further to Kinlochleven.

Walk No 2 Kinlochleven to Loch Ossian – 16 miles (25.75 kms)
There are several variations on walk No 1, one of which is to head
south-east at Lochtreighead and follow the track beside the railway
to the Allt Luib Ruaridh. Then turn left by the track to Loch Ossian
Youth Hostel, or keep alongside the railway to Corrour railway
station. The Youth Hostel is only open from the beginning of June
until the end of September – there is no store at this hostel and all
food must be carried.

Binnein Mor – 3,700 ft (1,127.5 m)
This is the highest mountain in the Mamore range. There is a path
from Kinlochleven which can be followed round the north-west side
of Meall an Doire Dharaich. The path crosses the track which leads
down to Kinlochleven from Loch Eilde Mor; continue on the path
flanking Na Gruagaichean until some lochans are reached. From
there the path peters out and you have to ascend steeply to the left

through rough quartzite scree to the saddle south of the top. The summit ridge runs north and south for about $\frac{1}{2}$ mile (0.81 kms), with the highest point at one end and the south top, 3,475 ft (1,058.9 m), at the other.

There are good views from the summit ridge; the Nevis massif to the north and the entire Mamore range to the west. Bidean nam Bian and other Glencoe giants can be seen to the south; Loch Leven and Loch Linnhe are to the south-west, with the hills of Ardgour beyond.

Loch Leven and Ardgour Hills (overleaf)

The final section of the West Highland Way starts from the most westerly houses at Kinlochleven. About $\frac{1}{4}$ mile (0.4 kms) along the A82, a signpost on the right-hand side of the road shows 'Public Footpath to Fort William'. After about 1 mile (1.61 kms) of steep ascent the path joins Caulfield's Military Road. This is the most direct access to the Military Road although there are other alternatives; for example, taking the very rough track which passes Mamore Lodge.

On reaching the old Military Road, follow its gradual ascent westwards above the north side of the Allt Nathrach. At the eastern end of Beinn na Cailleach, a magnificent panorama opens out as you look down from a height of about 800 ft (243 m) to Loch Leven surrounded by high and massive hills. As you continue on the track, the hills rise steeply to about 2,800 ft (853 m) on either side of the valley of the Allt Nathrach, and limit longer views. Stob Ban, 3,274 ft (998 m) now dominates the view; its upper slopes in certain lights look almost white, due to the loose scree of quartzite. From a distance, the quartzite is often mistaken for snow.

The house, Tigh-na-sleubhaich, is reached about 3 miles (4.83 kms) after you joined the old Military Road. This was formerly a stalker's house when the Mamore Forest was a famous deer forest. King Edward VII stalked part of it on several occasions. We are now on the summit of the track, at about 1,000 ft (305 m). The surface has been rough but from Tigh-na-sleubhaich for about 1 mile (1.61 kms) until you reach the ruined cottage, Lairigmor, the walking is softer – although in wet conditions the road becomes a watercourse.

At Lairigmor, the mountain to the south is Mam na Gualainn, 2,603 ft (794 m) and it dominates the view. On the south side of the glen here a path goes over the lower slopes of this hill to Callert on Loch Leven – about 3 miles (4.83 kms) away. It is a pleasant diversion, if you have time, to take this path to Callert and look across Loch Leven to Glencoe.

The Callert–Lairigmor path has been in dispute for a number of years but happily the situation is now resolved. The route is recorded in the Register of Sasines as a right of way, but now terminates to the west of Ferry Cottage on Loch Leven.

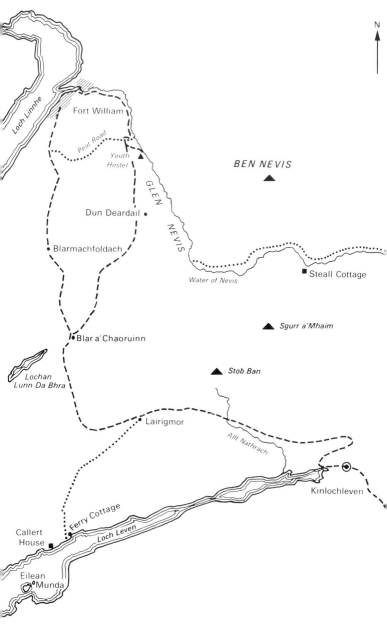

The islands of Loch Leven

Looking across Loch Leven from Callert, you will see several small islands towards the southern shore. The largest and most westerly one is called Eilean Munde and is named after St Fintan Mundus (or Mundu, or Munna), an Irish friend of St Columba who built a church on the island.

The first Christian missionary to come to Glencoe was St Kenneth, the Pictish monk, who later went to work in Fife. He chose a smaller island nearer to Ballachulish Bridge called Eilean Choinneich. It was a custom for those early missionaries to choose islands for their homes and churches. They were away from the dangers of war and the world, yet still accessible. Also the wolf survived in Scotland into the seventeenth century, and if the graves were on an island, they were safe from these beasts.

There are three landing-places on Eilean Munde called the Ports of the Dead: the island was used by the MacDonalds of Glencoe, the Stewarts of Ballachulish and the Camerons of Callert for burial and each had a recognised port. If for some reason a clan could not use its own port, the boat would return to the mainland and try again. The MacDonalds who were killed in the massacre of 1692 are said to have been buried there.

One of the islets near Eilean Munde is Eilean a'Chomhraidh, or the Isle of Discussion, a meeting place to discuss disputes on questions of land ownership, etc. When a dispute had been settled they would sail up to another islet, Eilean na Bainne, the Isle of Convenant or Ratification, where agreements were drawn up and sealed.

If you have a strong pair of binoculars you may see seals lying on the rocks. Swans still nest on the islands and there is a heronry.

The Ballachulish Figure

Not far from the islands at North Ballachulish, workmen trenching ground on 20 November 1880 unearthed a five-foot oaken statue of a nude female, which had been cut out of a log. The eyes were formed from small white quartz pebbles. The figure was at first believed to be that of a Norse pagan goddess, probably Freya (the equivalent of Venus). Now archaeologists think it is not Norse, but may be Scottish and date from the early centuries AD. It is known as the Ballachulish Figure and is housed in the National Museum of Antiquities of Scotland, in Edinburgh.

The West Highland Way continues from Lairigmor westwards for about a mile (1.61 kms) then turns north, ascending for a short distance to a spot height of 904 ft (275 m). Then the route descends gradually with the Allt na Lairige Moire on your left. Shortly before the track reaches the tarmac road at Blar a' Chaoruinn the surface becomes very rough. During the descent there are fine views towards Lochan Lunn Da Bhra. The distance from Lairigmor to Blar a' Chaoruinn is approximately 3 miles (4.83 kms) and at this point it finally parts company with Caulfield's old Military Road.

Lochan Lunn Da Bhra

Loch Lundavra (or to give it its Gaelic name, Lochan Lunn Da Bhra) stretches for about 1 mile (1.61 kms) and is about 500 ft (152 m) above sea-level in a hollow among the high hills of Mamore. The local folklore relates that it harboured a *tarbhuisge* (water bull) which emerged occasionally and grazed with other cattle in order to lure one of them to its watery home. On a little island in the Loch, Lulach, who was a cousin to Macbeth and his successor as king, is supposed to have resided. The Loch can be reached easily following the road to the left for about ½ mile (0.81 kms).

Lundavra to Fort William via Glen Nevis

The last stretch of the official West Highland Way branches off the road at Blar a' Chaoruinn and continues on a north-easterly course through a forestry plantation by the line of an old dyke. It emerges into open ground for a short distance before returning into the plantations. The route contours the rough slopes of Sgorr Chalum on the right, then turns towards the col on the left of Dun Deardail.

By this time, the mass of Ben Nevis has come into view, or – more accurately – the south-westerly aspect of Britain's highest mountain.

Loch Leven and the Pap of Glencoe

Dun Deardail – a vitrified hill-fort
Dun Deardail was originally thought to be one of a chain of watch-towers stretching from Oban to Strathpeffer, but this is now disputed by some archaeologists. It is a vitrified fort and scheduled as an Ancient Monument. These vitrified structures were supposed to have been the result of deliberate fusion by fire of timber-laced dry-stone buildings, which were built by the colonizing Celts from the first century BC until well into the post-Roman period. There is some doubt about ordinary fire having sufficient heating capacity to melt the silica in the stones, but no other explanation can be offered as to how these silicate compounds were fused.

The Way is now following a northerly course over the col and descends steeply through dense woods. Care should be taken, and it is advisable to follow the markers in this area. After a sharp zigzag descent, the Way joins a good forest road. Turn left, and this road descends gently into Glen Nevis. After approximately 1 mile (1.61 kms) this forestry road is joined by another track coming in from the right – those wishing to visit Glen Nevis Youth Hostel should take this right-hand track for a few hundred yards, and then turn left to join the public road. The hostel is situated a short distance up the Glen road.

The West Highland Way continues on the forest road for another $\frac{1}{2}$ mile (0.8 kms) and then turns right to join the public road. Turn left for Fort William, which is reached in approximately $2\frac{1}{2}$ miles (4 kms). The official route ends at Bridge of Nevis.

Lundavra to Fort William via Blarmachfoldach
A more direct alternative route to Fort William on the last stretch of the West Highland Way continues on the old Military Road, which is now a single-track tarmac road from Blar a' Chaoruinn. After $1\frac{1}{2}$ miles (2.41 kms), you reach the scattered crofting community of Blarmachfoldach. This little village was one of the last places in the

Junction of the Military Road and Lundavra Road
Lochan Lunn Da Bhra (overleaf)
En route to Blarmachfoldach (overleaf)

Highlands where the Old New Year – 12 January – was rigidly observed in preference to the usual New Year's Day – 1 January. This custom was carried out here from time immemorial, but came to an end in 1950 when the patriarch of the village died. As well as observing the Old New Year, the inhabitants of Blarmachfoldach did not observe British Summer Time, so their time could be an hour behind the rest of Britain. These old traditions have disappeared, and conformity now prevails.

Continue down the Lundavra road for about 2 miles (3.22 kms) until you approach the first houses of Fort William; there are some fine views over Loch Linnhe and the hills beyond. The road joins the main thoroughfare of the town about 100 yards (91 m) south of the Court House.

Fort William
Arrival at Fort William from Glasgow completes the West Highland Way. The population of the town is about 4,000 but in the summer months the number of visitors staying here can double this easily.

The name of the town is derived from the fort built during the seventeenth century to keep the Highland clans in check. It was named in honour of the King. The adjoining settlement, built by local inhabitants who wished to trade with the soldiers, was called Maryburgh after his consort and in keeping with the name of the fort. The name Maryburgh was superseded by Gordonsburgh, in honour of the Huntlys who were the landlords of the district. In 1834 the name of the town was again changed, to Duncansburgh, by Sir Duncan Cameron who became its landlord. Despite these different names, that of the fort has survived as the name of the town today.

In 1864 part of the barracks was demolished, some of the material being used for the construction of houses and the building of the old Belford Hospital. The later demolition by the West Highland Railway Company made room for their engine sheds. Demolition was renewed after the Second World War and nothing remains of the old fort.

Outskirts of Fort William and Loch Linnhe

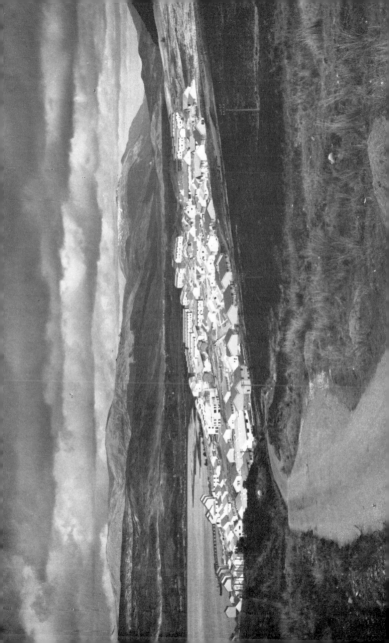

Fort William was the first town in Britain to have its streets and houses lit by electricity produced solely by means of its own water-power; the streets were first lit by electricity in 1896. The electricity supply of the town was controlled by a private company until 1937, when it was taken over by the Town Council; the control was transferred in 1947 to the North of Scotland Hydro-Electric Board.

The West Highland Museum in Cameron Square is well worth a visit. Many interesting Jacobite exhibits are kept there, as well as other objects of antiquarian interest. Of interest to all outdoor enthusiasts are the Visitors' Books from the hotel, which used to be on the summit of Ben Nevis.

Ben Nevis – 4,408 ft (1,344 m)
No apology is required for giving Ben Nevis a separate sub-section in this chapter. It was only in 1870 that 'The Ben' was surveyed and declared to be the highest mountain in Britain. Until 1964 its height was always given as 4,406 ft (1,343 m) but the Ordnance Survey announced that post-war triangulation and levelling had fixed its height as 4,408 ft (1,344 m).

There is some doubt about the origin of the name Nevis but it generally appears to mean 'venemous' or 'malicious' – a meaning which is quite apt as thick mist can come down suddenly, catching out people climbing it. Indeed 'The Ben' has gained an unpleasant reputation as a killer mountain. The first recorded ascent was made in the summer of 1771 by a certain James Robertson, who was commissioned to bring back botanical specimens from the Highland hills for the Edinburgh University Museum. Another botanist who made an early recorded ascent was James Dickson: his companion was Mungo Park, his brother-in-law and future explorer in Africa.

The Scottish Meteorological Society in 1877 considered the possibility of taking daily readings on the summit. A Mr Clement Wragge, an English scientist, climbed Ben Nevis every day during the summers of two successive years, 1881 and 1882, for the purpose of taking these observations. This is a unique record and his

Ben Nevis from Banavie

disregard for bad weather earned for him the nickname of 'Inclement Wragge'. What made this feat more remarkable was that in those days no track existed and the upper part of the climb had to be made over bare rock. It was mainly as a result of Wragge's work that plans were made to build a summit observatory.

A pony track was constructed first and then the small observatory, which was opened in 1883. It consisted originally of one apartment – a combined living-room and office. As so much trouble was experienced during the first winter with drifting snow, a larger room and two additional bedrooms and a tower were added during the next summer. It was connected first by telegraph and afterwards by telephone with a low-level observatory in Fort William. Continuous observations were made and the summit observatory remained in service until October 1904, when it was closed owing to lack of financial support.

Close to the observatory a hotel (as it was then called) was built, which was open from the beginning of June until the end of September each year. It was really a large timber hut with sleeping accommodation for about a dozen guests. It remained in service until the First World War, when it was closed. Gradually it fell into decay and was never re-opened.

Also on Ben Nevis is the Scottish Mountaineering Club hut, which was presented by Dr and Mrs W. Inglis Clark in memory of their son, captain Charles Inglis Clark, who died in 1918. It is situated at about 2,200 ft (670 m) close to the Allt a' Mhuilinn.

The ascent of Ben Nevis
The climb up Ben Nevis by the pony track is the ordinary route to the summit, and is more a test of endurance than a difficult climb. It is perfectly simple under the usual summer conditions but mist can descend very quickly and you should be properly clothed and shod even though the day starts with fine prospects. The track is very rough because it has not been kept in good repair since the observatory closed in 1904.

Leave Fort William by the north road and cross Nevis Bridge,

Ben Nevis from Corpach

taking the secondary road on the right to reach Achintee Farm, where the pony track starts. The track climbs across the steep slope of Meall an t-Suidhe and reaches the col between that top and Carn Dearg, above the Lochan Meall an t-Suidhe. Another path joins the pony track here on the left; this path has come up the Allt a'Mhuilinn which is another approach to 'The Ben'. If one has time it is worth going along this path for 1½ miles (2.4 kms) or so, because it gives good views of the northern precipices.

A short climb above the junction of the two paths at the lochan, there used to be the half-way hut, where observations were taken when the observatory was in service, but there is now no trace of it. At one time a toll of one shilling was collected for the pleasure of climbing Ben Nevis; the money was put to the cost of keeping the track in good repair. The climber was given a card in receipt and it was not considered complete until he had this card stamped 'Ben Nevis Summit' with the date.

As the track zigzags up the scree-covered slopes it becomes very rough and the ascent is steeper. On approaching the plateau summit the path is near the precipices, and as some of the gullies extend far into the plateau it is as well to keep a sharp lookout in misty weather; in winter and spring special care should be taken as large cornices of snow may project many feet over the edge.

If you are staying at the Youth Hostel in Glen Nevis, the route can be shortened by crossing the bridge on the River Nevis and going straight up the slope of Meall an t-Suidhe to join the pony track close to the first zigzag.

Allow about four to five hours for the ascent from Achintee to the summit in summer, and about three hours for the descent.

There are likely to be patches of snow on the bare and windswept summit even if you left a scorching summer day down below. If the atmosphere is clear, you will be rewarded for the hard slog of the climb with a tremendous panorama at the top. An indicator on the summit helps identify the numerous mountains, lochs and islands. The Cairngorms are about 50 miles (80.5 kms) to the east; to the south are Ben More and Stobinian, Bauchaille Etive Mor, and

Glen Nevis Youth Hostel

Beinn Laoigh. Again further to the south and westwards the islands
are predominant – Arran, Jura, Colonsay, Mull, Coll with Tiree
behind it. North-westwards further mainland peaks and groups
beckon – the Kintail hills and a glimpse of Torridon. The farthest
view of all in the whole panorama to the left of Jura – if the weather
is absolutely clear – is the coast of Ireland 120 miles (193 kms) away.

I can only hope you choose a good clear day for the climb. From
old observatory records it is calculated that one day out of six is
clear on the summit and that April is usually the best month for
clear weather.

The Ben Nevis Race

How would you like to *run* up and down Ben Nevis? This is what
actually happens in Britain's toughest athletic event. The Ben Nevis
Race is always held on the first Saturday of September.

It began officially in 1895 when William Swan, a local barber, ran
all the way up and down the mountain from the old post office in the
High Street, in 2 hours 41 minutes. From then until the closing of
the observatory in 1904, the race was held annually. The event was
revived in 1937 and is open to all amateur athletes from Britain and
overseas.

The present record is 1 hour, 38 minutes, 50 seconds for the
completion of the race from the starting-point in the old King
George V Park on the outskirts of Fort William. This record was set
up in 1964 by an Englishman, Peter Hall from Barrow, who enjoys
this added distinction of being the only man who has ever won the
race four times. With the moving of the starting-point now to the
new town park at Claggan, a new record will have to be established,
as the road to the foot of 'The Ben' is now shorter.

The race consists of a 2-mile (3.22 kms) road-run to the foot of
the mountain. This is followed by 5 miles (8.05 kms) of pony track
from about 100 ft (30 m) above sea-level to 4,408 ft (1,344 m). The
descent involves an entirely different set of muscles and a different
technique, and this is followed by the road run back to the finishing-
post.

Glen Nevis

The race has developed from a rather haphazard local affair into a major athletic event and is supervised most efficiently by the Ben Nevis Race Committee. As there can be over 200 competitors taking part annually, it is no mean achievement not only to organise the competition but to provide the necessary safety precautions. All the competitors have to sign a declaration that they are medically fit before they set off and the progress of the runners is checked all the way up and down the mountain.

Accommodation and transport

The town of Fort William has many hotels, boarding-houses and private houses which provide bed and breakfast; there is also the Youth Hostel in Glen Nevis which is open all year and has 120 beds. A caravan and camping site in Glen Nevis can accommodate over 450 pitches. Although a lot of accommodation is available, remember the town is extremely busy with tourists and in the height of summer very often there is not a bed available for miles. So it is advisable to book well beforehand.

The Fort William and District Tourist Organization is located at the Railway Station, Fort William (telephone 0397–3781) and gives details of accommodation, places of interest and has a wide range of publications. There is a rail service from Fort William to Glasgow and further south, and it is also the starting-point for buses to other parts of the Highlands.

Suggestions for additional walks and climbs in this section

Glen Nevis

The approach to Glen Nevis from Fort William is exactly the same as was described for the ascent of Ben Nevis. The Glen itself, however, is worth exploring further as it is one of the finest in Scotland and its upper reaches have been described as Himalayan in

Steall waterfall, Upper Glen Nevis

Polldubh Falls, Glen Nevis (overleaf)

Sgurr a'Mhaim and Stob Ban, in the Mamores, from Glen Nevis (overleaf)

character. A well-surfaced road winds into the Glen from Fort William for about 5 miles (8.05 kms). It crosses the river at Achriabhach and continues as a single-traffic road with passing places, for another 2 miles (3.22 kms). Beyond the car park the Glen is traversed by a rough track for walkers only. It keeps high along a steep hillside for about ½ mile (0.81 kms) and then turns south for a little over another ½ mile (0.81 kms) where it passes through the magnificent gorge.

The track follows the Water of Nevis and passes Steall Cottage, the club hut of the Lochaber Mountaineering Club, on the south side of the river from the track. Near the vicinity of the cottage is the magnificent waterfall of An Steall Bhan, meaning 'the white gush' – it is more of a spout than a broad waterfall. Most walkers who wish to return to Fort William turn here, but the cross-country enthusiast can continue another 8 miles (12.88 kms) through the Glen to its head near Loch Treig. It is wiser to do this during a spell of dry weather, for frequent streams must be crossed and it can be very marshy. In places the track has disappeared.

The Mamores

Attractions such as Ben Nevis keep the walker and climber away from the Mamores, but they are worthy of exploration in themselves. The peaks of the Mamores cannot be assessed properly until you are well up towards the tops, with the exception of Sgurr a'Mhaim. The second highest peak in the group, its huge bulk appears to block the exit from Glen Nevis as you come up the lower part of the Glen past Achintee and the Youth Hostel.

The group consists of about fifteen tops above the 3,000 ft (914 m) contour, concentrated in a roughly rectangular area some 4 miles (6.44 kms) north and south, about 7 miles (11.27 kms) east and west, with Loch Leven to the south and Glen Nevis in the north. The main east-west ridge is narrow and sends off three spurs to the north from which one can survey, as from a grandstand, the breadth of the Ben Nevis massif.

For those who can only devote a day or a couple of days to the Mamores, the ascent either of Sgurr a'Mhaim or Stob Ban from Glen Nevis is a 'must'. For either peak the start is made from

Polldubh, roughly where the road crosses the Water of Nevis.

Sgurr a'Mhaim – 3,601 ft (1,097 m)
Walk up the Allt Coire a'Mhusgain to the col and then turn left to
reach Sgor an Iubhair. Turn left again and cross the ridge which
leads to the summit. The view due north is the most dramatic
spectacle provided by the Mamores: Ben Nevis and its
accompanying peaks.

Stob Ban – 3,274 ft (977.6 m)
The top is generally ascended by its north ridge from Polldubh but it
is interesting to follow the route as for Sgurr a'Mhaim to the col as
there are good views of its precipitous buttresses; turn right at the
col and a rough scramble up the quartzite scree brings you to the
cairn.

From the slopes of Stob Ban you can look down the whole length
of lower Glen Nevis from Polldubh to Bridge of Nevis, and as you
rise higher there comes into view the distant prospect of the peaks
away to the north-west, beyond the bounds of Lochaber and on the
fringes of Knoydart itself. Southward there is a fine panorama of
the Glencoe peaks.

The following list of Gaelic names and their meanings include some of the important mountains and other features shown on Ordnance maps. The spellings have been taken from the One-Inch Ordnance Survey Maps; the reader should note that in many cases the names and spellings are corrupted from the original Gaelic and sometimes are only of local significance.

A'Bhuidheanach	yellow ridge
A'Chailleach	old wife
A'Chrois	the cross
Airgiod	silver
Allt, Abhainn	mountain stream or river
Am Binnein (Stobinian)	the pinnacle
Am Bodach	the old man
An Caisteal	the castle
An Cearcallach	the hoop
An Creachan	the rock
An Garbhanach	the rough ridge
An Gearannach	the short ridge
An Sgor	the rocky peak
An Stuc	the steep rock
An t-Sron	the nose
Aonach	upland moor
Aonach Beag	little ridge
Aonach Dubh	black ridge
Aonach Eagach	notched ridge
Aonach Mor	great ridge
Auch	meadow
Avon	large stream or river
Bad	small clump of trees
Ban	white, pale or fair
Bealach	col, pass
Bealach-eadar-dha-Beinn	the pass between the mountains
Bealach nan Corp	the pass of the corpses
Bealach a'Mhaim	the pass on the ridge

Beg, Bheag	small, little
Ben, Beinn, Bheinn	mountain (general name)
Beinn Achaladair	the mountain of the mower
Beinn Alder	mountain of rock and water
Beinn Bheag	the little mountain
Beinn a'Bheithir	peak of the thunder-bolt or monster
Beinn Bheoil	mountain in front (of Ben Alder)
Beinn Bhreac	the mottled mountain
Beinn Bhuidhe	the yellow mountain
Beinn a'Bhuiridh	hill of roaring (stags)
Beinn Chabhair	the mountain of the antler
Beinn a'Chaisteal	the mountain of the castle
Beinn Chaluim	Malcolm's mountain
Beinn a'Chaoruinn	mountain of the rowan tree
Beinn Cheathaich	the mountain of mists
Beinn a'Chlachair	mason's mountain
Beinn a'Chochuill	mountain of the hood
Beinn Chonzie	the mountain of the cry of the deer
Beinn a'Chreachain	the mountain of the clam shell
Beinn a'Chuallaich	mountain of herding
Beinn Chumhainn	narrow mountain
Beinn a' Chuirn	the mountain of the rocky heap
Beinn Chuachan	mountain of peaks or stacks
Beinn Donich	the brown mountain
Beinn Dorain	the mountain of the otter
Beinn an Dothaidh	the mountain of scorching
Beinn Dubh	the black mountain
Beinn Dubhain	the mountain of the black burn
Beinn Dubhchraig	the mountain of the black rock
Beinn Each (Beinn nan Eachan)	the mountain of the horses
Beinn Eibhinn	mountain with a fair outlook
Beinn Eunaich	fowling peak

Beinn Fhada	long mountain
Beinn Fhionnlaidh	Finlay's mountain
Beinn Ghlas	the grey mountain
Beinn Iaruinn	iron mountain
Ben Ime	the butter mountain
Ben Ledi	the mountain of the gentle slope
Beinn an Lochain	the mountain of the little loch
Ben Lomond	the beacon mountain
Ben Lui (Laoigh)	the mountain of the calf
Beinn Maol Chaluim	Calum's bare mountain
Beinn a' Mhanach	the monk's mountain
Beinn Mhic-Mhonaidh	mountain of the son of the moor
Beinn Mholach	shaggy mountain
Beinn More (Mhor)	the big mountain
Beinn na Lap	boggy mountain
Beinn nan Aighean	mountain of the hinds
Beinn nan Oighreag	the mountain of the cloudberries
Ben Nevis	venomous, malicious mountain
Beinn Odhar	the dun-coloured mountain
Ben Oss	the mountain of the elk
Beinn Ruadh	the red mountain
Ben Starav	strong or stout mountain
Beinn Tharsuinn	the oblique mountain
Beinn Trilleachan	mountain of sandpipers
Beinn an t-Sithein	the hill of the fairy knoll
Beinn Tulaichean	the knolly mountain
Beinn Udlaidh	the dark (gloomy) mountain
Beinn Udlamain	mountain of the unsteady place
Ben Vane	the white mountain
Ben Venue	the mountain of the caves
Bharraig	mountain slope
Bidean nam Bian	pinnacle of the hides

Binnean Mor	big hill
Brae	slope
Breac	brown-spotted, piebald
Buachaille	herdsman or shepherd
Buachaille Etive Beag	the little herdsman of Etive
Buachaille Etive Mor	the great herdsman of Etive
Buidhe	golden yellow
Caber	deer antlers
Cadha	narrow pass or ravine at side or foot of mountain
Cailleach	old woman
Cairn (Carn)	heap of stones (often marking summit of hill)
Caisteal	the castle
Caochan	small stream
Caol	slender, thin or narrow
Carn Ban	white cairn
Carn Beag Dearg	little red cairn
Carn Beallach	cairn of the pass
Carn a' Chuilinn	cairn of the holly
Carn Dearg	red cairn
Carn Dearg Meadhonach	middle red cairn
Carn Easgann Bana	cairn of the white eels
Carn an Fhreiceadain	cairn of the watcher
Carn Gorm	the blue cairn
Carn Liath	grey cairn
Carn Meirg	the rust-coloured cairn
Carn Mor Dearg	big red cairn
Carn na Laraiche Maoile	cairn of the bare site, or ruin
Carn na Saobhaide	cairn of the fox's den
Carn Sgulain	cairn of the basket
Carraigean	projecting rocks or pillars
Cas	steep
Cath	battle
Ceann Garbh	the rough head
Chalamain	pigeon

Chno Dearg	red nut
Ciste	coffin
Clach	stone, boulder
Clach Bheinn	the stony mountain
Clach Leathad	stone slope
Cnoc	little hill, knoll or hillock
Cnoc Coinnich	the mossy hillock
Coille (Coile)	wood or forest
Coillessan	the wood of the waterfalls
Coire (Corrie)	cirque, glaciated rocky amphitheatre
Coiregrogain	the awkward corrie
Coire Daimh	the corrie of the stags
Coire Gaothaich	the corrie of the winds
Coire Cheathaich	the corrie of mists
Craig (Creag)	crag or rocky hill
Creach Bheinn	mountain of prey or spoil
Creag na Caillich	the crag of the old woman
Creag Dubh	black rock
Creag Mhor	the big crag
Creag Pitridh	rock of the hollow places
Creag Tharsuinn	the oblique crag
Croft (croit)	small piece of arable land or small farm
Crom	crooked, bent or curved
Cruach Ardrain	the high heap
Cruach Innse	stack of the meadow
Curra Lochain	the marshy lochan
Dail (Dell)	flood plain of river
Darach	oak wood
Dearg	red, brownish red
Diollaid a' Chairn	saddle of the cairn
Doire	thicket or clump of trees
Domhain	deep or profound
Drochaid Glas	grey bridge
Drum (Druim)	ridge or spur

Dubh	black or dark
Eag	rocky notch or gap
Eas	waterfall
Eilein	island
Elrig	deer trap
Etchachen	junipers
Faradh	ladder
Feith	peat hags, bog or fen
Faicaill	saw-edged ridge
Fionn	white, pale or lilac
Fionn Choirein	the fair corrie
Fraochaidh	place of heather
Fuaran	spring, source of river
Gall	stranger, especially lowlanders
Gamhna	stirks, steers or young bullocks
Garbh	rough, also thick
Garbh Bheinn	rough mountain
Garbh Mheall	the rough hump
Geadas	pike
Geal	white, clear or bright
Geal-Charn	white cairn
Geal-Charn Mor	big white cairn
Gearr Aonach	short height or ridge
Ginthsach	pine forest
Glac	narrow valley, cut or defile
Glas	greenish-grey
Glas Bheinn	grey mountain
Glas Bheinn Mor	big grey mountain
Glen, Gleann	narrow, enclosed valley, high ground on each side
Gorm	blue (azure) or green (grassy)
Inch (Innis)	pasture (for cattle)

Inver	confluence of waters, or mouth of stream
Iolair	eagle
Laggan (Lagan)	little hollow
Lairig, Lairige, Learg	mountain pass
Laogh	calf
Leathann	broad
Leum an Eireannaich	Irishman's leap
Leum Uilleim	William's leap
Liath	whitish-grey or grey
Loch	inland lake, also arm of sea (fjord)
Loch Achray	the loch of the level field
Loch Ard	the high loch
Lochan nan Cat	the little loch of the cat
Lochan na Lairige	the little loch of the pass
Loisgte	burned
Lyn (Laun)	enclosed meadow
Mam	large round hill
Mam Coire Easain	moor, or plateau of the corrie of the waterfalls
Mam na Gualaiun	plateau of the shoulder
Meall	shapeless hill or lump
Meall Bhuidhe	the rounded yellow hill
Meall a' Bhuiridh	hill of the roaring (stags)
Meall a' Choire Leith	the round hill of the grey corrie
Meall a' Churain	the round hill of the stones
Meall Corranaich	the round hill of the corrie of bracken
Meall Cruidh	hill of the shoe
Meall Cuanail	hill facing the sea
Meall Dearg	red hill
Meall Dubh	the round black hill
Meall Garbh	rough hill

Meall Glas	the round grey hill
Meall Greign	the round hill of the cheek
Meall Liath	the grey lump
Meall Luaidhe	the round hill of lead
Meall na h-Aisre	hill of the defile
Meall na Leitreach	hill of slopes
Meall nan Eun	hill of the birds
Meall an t-Seallaidhe	the round hill of the sight
Meall an t-Snaim	hill of the knot
Meall nan Tarmachan	the round hill of the ptarmigan
Meirleach	cattle thieves or raiders
Mhareaidh	associated with horses
Moine	moss or bog
Monadh	mountain (plateau type)
Mor	large, big
Mullach Coire an Iubhair	top of the corrie of the yew tree
Mullach Coire Choille-rais	top of the corrie of the shrub wood
Mullach Coire nan Nead	top of the corrie of the nests
Mullach nan Coirean	top of the corries
Na Gruagaichean	the maidens
Nathrach	viper or adder
Odhar	dun, drab or yellowish
Ord	hill or steep round form, rather isolated
Preis	thicket or bush
Reidh	field
Riach	yellowish or brownish grey
Rowchoish (Rudha a'Chois)	the point of the hollow
Ruadh	bright red

Ry, Ruighe or Raidh	shieling (seasonal grazing and settlement)
Sgairaich	scree slopes
Sgairneach Mhor	big rocky hillside
Sgiath Chuil	the back wing
Sgor	sharp steep hill or small steep crag
Sgor Choinnich	Kenneth's peak
Sgor Gaibhre	peak of the goats
Sgor Iutharn	hell's peak
Sgor na h-Ulaidh	peak of the hidden treasure
Sgor nam Fiannaidh	peak of the Fianns
Sgor an Inbhair	peak of the yew tree
Sgor Bhann	white peak
Sgor Dhearg	red peak
Sgor Dhonuill	Donald's peak
Sgurr a' Bhuic	peak of the buck
Sgurr a' Mhaim	peak of the pass
Sgurr Choinnich Beag	little mossy peak
Sgurr Choinnich Mor	big mossy peak
Sgurr Eilde Beag	little crag of the hinds
Sgurr Eilde Mor	big crag of the hinds
Sgurr Innse	peak of the meadow
Sleamhuinn	smooth
Sluggan	gorge
Sneachda	snow
Sneachdach Slinnean	snowy shoulder-blade
Sputen	small waterfall or spout
Sron	spur linking mountains to strath
Sron a' Ghearrain	nose of the gelding
Sron an Isean	nose of the young bird, or chick
Sron Coire nah-Iolaire	nose of the eagle's corrie
Sron Garbh	rough nose
Sron Garbh Choire	nose of the rough corrie

Sron nan Guibhas	nose of the firs
Stac	steep, high cliff or pinnacle
Steall	cascade
Stob	peak, point or spur
Stob a' Bhruaich Leith	peak of the grey brae
Stob a' Choin	the dog's point
Stob a' Choire Leith	peak of the grey corrie
Stob a' Choire Mheadhoin	peak of the middle corrie
Stob a' Choire Odhair	peak of the dun corrie
Stob Coire an Lochain	the peak of the corrie of the little loch
Stob Creagach	the rocky point
Stob a' Ghlais Choire	peak of the grey corrie
Stob an Aonaich Mhor	peak of the big ridge
Stob an Cul Choire	peak at the back of the corrie
Stob an Eas	the point of the waterfall
Stob an Fhir-Bhoga	the spur of the bowman
Stob an Fhuarain	peak of the well
Stob Ban	white peak
Stob Choire Dhuibh	peak of the black corrie
Stob Coir' an Albannaich	peak of the corrie of the Scotsman
Stob Coire Altruim	peak of the nursing corrie (hinds with calves)
Stob Coire a' Chairn	peak of the stony corrie
Stob Coire an Easain	peak of the corrie of the waterfalls
Stob Coire an Fhir Dhuibh	peak of the corrie of the black man
Stob Coire an Laoigh	peak of the corrie of the calf
Stob Coire Bhealaich	peak of the corrie of the pass
Stob Coire Cath na Sine	peak of the corrie of the battle
Stob Coire Dheirg	peak of the red corrie
Stob Coire Gaibhre	peak of the corrie of the goats
Stob Coire Leith	peak of the grey corrie
Stob Coire nam Beith	peak of the corrie of the birch trees

Stob Coire na Ceannain	peak of the corrie of the bluff
Stob Coire nan Lochain	peak of the corrie of the lochans
Stob Coire Raineach	peak of the corrie of the ferns
Stob Coire Sgreamhach	peak of the rocky corrie
Stob Dearg	red peak
Stob Diamh (Daimh)	peak of the stags
Stob Dubh	black peak
Stob Garbh	rough peak
Stob Ghabhar	peak of the goats
Stob na Broige	peak of the shoe
Stob na Doire	peak of the copse
Strath	broad, open valley
Stuc a' Chroin	the peak of the cloven foot
Stuchd an Lochain	the peak of the little loch
Suim	rounded
Tionail	assembly or gathering
Tom	round hillock or knoll
Tom Molach	the tufty hillock
Tom na Sroine	hill of the nose
Tor, Torr	conical hill or rock outcrop on rising ground
Toul	barn
Tullach (Tulach)	green cultivated hill
Uaine	bright green
Uamh Bheag	the little cave
Uinneag a' Ghlas Choire	window of the grey corrie
Uisge	water

The word has come to mean the distinctive woollen cloth in which coloured threads are woven into both weft and warp at intervals to give a chequered or cross-striped effect, some patterns being so closely associated with a certain Scottish family or clan as to be regarded as their exclusive property.

The theory that distinctive clan or family tartans date from a period earlier than the seventeenth century cannot be supported by historical evidence. The use of chequered and striped cloths by primitive peoples is natural; the wool of the black sheep woven in a pattern of stripes or squares into the wool of the white sheep is the simplest form of decorative weaving and it is this effect that is known as 'shepherd's plaid'. In the later Middle Ages, cheap striped woollen cloth, which was imported from North Africa and was the usual wear of Carmelite monks, was forbidden by the Pope because by that time it brought ridicule on the order. This cloth has remained a part of the general wear of the Arab peoples.

Striped materials have often formed a part of European fashion, but it is only in Scotland that the systematic weaving of chequered cloths has taken on a special significance, and from surviving pieces it can be seen that the earlier tartans were often very elaborate in the arrangement of their colours. They were also quite different in colour from modern tartans (though not necessarily less bright) as only vegetable dyes were used.

In the late eighteenth century, military tartans came to be designed for the Highland regiments. This largely military revival of tartan led in the nineteenth century to a general interest that produced an imaginative and systematic recording of clan tartans (lacking in authenticity) by authors and artists, creating what has been called 'the great tartan myth'. Intermittent efforts to explode the myth in the interest of historic truth have failed and the combined efforts of artists, writers, manufacturers and tailors have firmly established tartan as a Scottish clan badge.

Identification of the clan to which a Highlander belonged was not so much what tartan he was wearing as what piece of natural material he stuck in his bonnet or attached to other parts of his attire. He also shouted his clan slogan in battle, again as a means of identification.

A list of clans with their badges and slogans, where known, is shown in Appendix 3.

Badges and slogans of the ancient clans

Name	Badge	Slogan
Brodie	periwinkle	
Buchanan	bilberry or oak	Clar Innis (an island on Loch Lomand)
Cameron	oak or crowberry	Chianna nan con Thigibh a so's gheibh sich feoil (Sons of the hounds come here and get flesh)
Campbell	wild myrtle or fir club moss	Cruachan (a mountain near Loch Awe)
Chisholm	fern	—
Colquhoun	dogberry or hazel	Cnoc ealachain (hill of the hearth)
Cumming	wheat	—
Drummond	wild thyme or holly	—
Farquharson	Scots fir	Carn na Cuimhue (Stone of Remembrance)
Forbes	broom	Lonach (a mountain in Strathdon)
Fraser	yew	Caisteal dhuni (Castle Dounie)
Gordon	ivy	A Gordon, A Gordon
Graham	laurel	—
Grant	pine tree	Stand fast Cregallachie
Hay	mistletoe	A Hay, A Hay
Home	broom	A Home, A Home
MacLennan	furze	Drum nan deur (the ridge of tears)
MacArthur	wild myrtle or fir club moss	Eisa, o'Eisa (Listen, oh listen)
MacDonald of Clanranald	common heath	Dh'aindeoin co theiradh e (Gainsay who dare)
MacDonald of Sleat	heath	Fraoch Eilean (the heathery isle)
MacDonnell of Glengarry	common heath	Creagen an Fhitlich (the raven's rock)
MacDonnel of Keppoch	heath	Dia is Naomh Aindrea (God and St Andrew)
MacDougall	bell heath or cypress	Buaidh no bas (Victory or death)
MacFarlane	cranberry or cloudberry	Loch Sloigh (Loch Sloy)
MacFie	oak or crowberry	—
Macgillivray	red whortleberry	Dunmaglass

Macgregor	pine tree	Ard Choille (high wood)
MacKay	reed grass and bullrush	Bratach bhan chlaun alidh (The white banner of the MacKays)
MacKenzie	holly	Tulach ard (A mountain in Kintail)
MacKinnon	pine tree	Cuimhuich bas Ailpen (Remember the death of Alpin)
MacIntosh and Clan Chattan	red whortleberry	Loch Moigh (loch of the plain)
MacLaren	laurel	Creag an turic (the boar's rock)
MacNaughton	trailing azalea	Fraoch eilean (heathery isle, Loch Awe)
MacPherson	white heath	Creag dhubh chloinn chatain (black craig of Clan Chattan)
MacRae	fir club moss	Sgur main (a mountain in Kintail)
Menzies	menzies heath	Geal is dearg a suas (Up with the white and red)
Munroe	common moss	Casteal folais'n a theine (Castle Foulis ablaze)
Robertson	five-leaved heath or bracken	Garg'n uair dhuisgear (Fierce when roused)
Stewart of Appin	oak or thistle	Creag an sgairbh (the cormorant's rock)

Appendix 4
James Macpherson and the Ossian legend

James Macpherson was born at Ruthven near Kingussie in 1738 and went to the local school before going on to King's College in Aberdeen. He returned to his native village as a teacher and started writing poetry. At the age of twenty he published a poem, 'The Highlander'. In 1760 appeared 'Fragments of Ancient Poetry collected in the Highlands of Scotland, and translated from the Gaelic or Erse language.'

By this time the young writer's fame had spread far beyond his native glen and a fund was raised to enable him to continue his researches. So the translations from the Celtic hero bard of the fifth century AD, known as Ossian, were given to the world in 'Fingal, An Ancient Poem' in six books, and 'Temora, An Ancient Poem' in eight books, in the course of 1762 and 1763.

These literary works created a sensation – they were all the rage in London; they were translated into most European languages and were greatly admired on the continent, in particular by Goethe, and Napoleon. He carried a volume of Ossian as part of his campaign luggage and it was a bedside companion in his lonely exile in St Helena. The Kings of Sweden took the name of Oscar from the poems and introduced it to their dynasty.

The authenticity of the poems was doubted by many, including Dr Johnson who challenged Macpherson to produce the originals. Macpherson is said to have fabricated what he did produce and to have inserted passages of his own. However, the idea that the tales were fabrications without foundation is incorrect, as Macpherson's command of the Gaelic language was not very good. Johnson's accusations so angered Macpherson that the latter threatened the worthy doctor with personal violence, and Dr Johnson deemed it prudent to buy a big stick with which to defend himself against a possible attack in the streets.

Macpherson made a modest fortune from his 'translations'; he died in 1796 and is buried in the Poets' Corner of Westminster Abbey.

The Clarsach

The clarsach, or Highland harp, is Scotland's oldest musical instrument. Brought over from Gaul to England before the birth of Christ, its use spread to Wales, Scotland and Ireland. From the sixth century AD Irish missionaries encouraged what local talent existed in Scotland, because the Irish players were famous both as teachers and instrument-makers. W.F. Skene, the Celtic historian, mentions a sculptured pillar on which an armed figure playing on the harp is seated – the pillar is believed to date from the ninth century. By the twelfth century, Scotland seems to have gained the lead in technique.

In the middle ages royalty learned to play the harp, and until the middle of the eighteenth century, harpers were employed at Court, by the Church, by clan chiefs and in noble families. They had a good social standing and were usually given a house and land. There were also wandering harpers, who were bearers of folk-tales, ballads and gossip. Harpers accompanied troops into battle until the harp was superseded by the pipes in the sixteenth century. By the mid-eighteenth century the clarsach had declined in popularity. The causes of its eventual disuse included the fact that other instruments becoming available were easier to learn, such as the clavichord and spinet; there was also the fanatical zeal of the Reformers, who ordered harps to be burnt at the market places as they considered them instruments of Satan. The bagpipe with its shrill martial music became more popular with the Highlanders.

The style of the Highland airs suited the clarsach, for the music of the Gaels is remarkable for its simplicity, wildness and pathos. The scale is different from the ordinary or diatonic scale, and is defective, wanting the fourth and the seventh, but, in the words of Skene, 'This very defect gives rise to the pleasing simplicity and plaintiveness of the Highland melody, and imparts to their music a character peculiarly adapted to the nature of their poetry'.

Today there is a revival of this old instrument and the clarsach is heard occasionally on the BBC, at festivals and concerts.

DARLING, F.F., and MORTON BOYD, J., *The Highlands and Islands*, London, Collins, 1964

DARLING, F. F., *West Highland Survey*, Oxford University Press, 1955

GRIMBLE, I., *The Trial of Patrick Sellar* (the story of the Evictions), London, Routledge & Kegan Paul, 1962

HALDANE, A. R. B., *The Drove Roads of Scotland*, London, Nelson, 1952

HARDY, ERIC, *A Guide to the Birds of Scotland*, London, Constable, 1978

HILLABY, JOHN, *Journey through Britain*, London, Constable, 1968

MACINNES, HAMISH, *Scottish Climbs*, London, Constable, 1971

MURRAY, W.H., *The Companion Guide to the West Highlands of Scotland*, London, Collins, 1972

PEARSALL, W. H., *Mountains and Moorland*, London, Collins, 1965

POUCHER, W. A., *The Scottish Peaks*, London, Constable, 1965

PRIOR, R., *Living with Deer*, London, Andre Deutsch, 1965

RAVEN, J., and WALTERS, M., *Mountain Flowers*, London, Collins, 1965

WEIR, TOM, *The Scottish Lochs*, London, Constable, 1980

Index